# When's GOD Gonna Show Up?

## Daily Discoveries of the Divine

Marge Fenelon

*Foreword by Archbishop Timothy M. Dolan*

Liguori
LIGUORI, MISSOURI

Imprimi Potest:
Thomas D. Picton, C.Ss.R.
Provincial, Denver Province
The Redemptorists

Imprimatur:
Archbishop Timothy M. Dolan
Archdiocese of Milwaukee, April 1, 2009

Published by Liguori Publications
Liguori, Missouri
To order, call 800-325-9521
www.liguori.org

**Library of Congress Cataloging-in-Publication Data**

Fenelon, Marge.
    When's God gonna show up? : daily discoveries of the divine / Marge Fenelon ; foreword by Timothy M. Dolan.—1st ed.
      p. cm.
    ISBN 978-0-7648-1832-5
    1. Catholic women—Prayers and devotions. 2. Church year meditations.
I. Title.
    BX2170.W7.F46 2009
    242'.802--dc22

2009013072

Unless otherwise noted, Scripture citations are from the New Revised Standard Version of the Bible, copyright 1989 by the Division of Christian Education of the National Council of Churches of Christ in the USA. All rights reserved. Used with permission.

Excerpts from *Vatican Council II: The Basic Sixteen Documents*, edited by Austin Flannery, OP, copyright © 1996 by Reverend Austin Flannery, OP. All rights reserved. Reprinted with permission of Costello Publishing Company.

Excerpts from English translation of the *Catechism of the Catholic Church* for the United States of America © 1994, United States Catholic Conference, Inc.—Libreria Editrice Vaticana; English translation of the *Catechism of the Catholic Church: Modifications from the Editio Typica* © 1997, United States Catholic Conference, Inc.—Libreria Editrice Vaticana.

Excerpts from John Paul II, Apostolic Letter *Salvifici Doloris*, Feb. 11, 1984. Copyright © 1984 Libreria Editrice Vaticana; Encyclical Letter *Redemptoris Mater*, March 25, 1987. Copyright © Libreria Editrice Vaticana.

Excerpt from John A. Hardon, S.J., *The Question and Answer Catholic Catechism* (New York: Doubleday, Image). © 1981 by John A. Hardon.

Excerpt by Thomas Merton, from NEW SEEDS OF CONTEMPLATION, copyright ©1961 by The Abbey of Gethsemani, Inc. Reprinted by permission of New Directions Publishing Corp.

Liguori Publications, a nonprofit corporation, is an apostolate of the Redemptorists. To learn more about the Redemptorists, visit Redemptorists.com.

Printed in the United States of America
13 12 11 10 09  5 4 3 2 1
First edition

To Fenelon Clan
I put my hands to the keyboard,
but you gave me the inspiration.

# Table of Contents

■ I I I I ■ I I I I ■ I I I I ■ I I I I ■ I I I I ■ I I I ■

# Foreword

■ ■ ■ ■ ■ ■ ■ ■ ■ ■ ■ ■ ■ ■ ■ ■ ■ ■ ■ ■ ■ ■ ■ ■ ■ ■ ■ ■ ■ ■ ■

WE HERE IN THE Archdiocese of Milwaukee are proud to claim as our patron, after Saint John the Evangelist, Saint Francis de Sales. In his ever-timely classic, *Introduction to the Devout Life,* Saint Francis de Sales makes a point so simple it is downright profound and usually overlooked: every one of us, in whatever state or stage of life, is called to virtue, perfection, and holiness. This summons—what the Second Vatican Council would term the *universal call to holiness*—is for all of us, not just our wonderful cloistered nuns or our devoted monks. There is no escaping the mandate of Jesus to be a saint!

The insight of Saint Francis de Sales needs continual re-articulation. The Little Flower did it in a legendary way, didn't she? And, although she will blush to be included in such company, my friend, Margaret Fenelon, does it for us today in this engaging work.

Marge would be the first to confess that she's no saint—which, by the way, only confirms my hunch that she's on the path to holiness!— but she enchants us all with homey, perceptive meditations on the mystery, mercy, presence, and power of God in our day-to-day lives. She can spot the divine, as you'll soon discover, in the comments of her wonderful kids, in the tensions of life, in the sadness and sickness of others. This is really a reflection on the Incarnation, that God has taken flesh, that he is here with us.

That Margaret would sense God's presence all around surprises me not at all. Not only is she a faithful Catholic, but she is a devoted member of Schoenstatt, whose charism points to a God so tender, so accessible, so available, so human, that he is most obvious as a baby in the arms of his blessed Mother or under the appearances of bread in the holy Eucharist.

If God can show up in a baby or in bread, he can show up anywhere. Our challenge is to recognize him. Open this book and let Margaret guide us!

MOST REVEREND TIMOTHY M. DOLAN
ARCHBISHOP OF MILWAUKEE

# Introduction

I REMEMBER Luke's first experience with eucharistic adoration. He was just four, Matthew was nine, Monica was six, and John was not yet born. In spite of our best efforts to explain the mystery before us, Luke completely missed the point, and the presence. His patience finally wore thin and, to our exasperation and embarrassment, he suddenly blurted out, "When's God gonna show up?"

How can it be that, like little Luke, we miss the times God shows up in *our* lives even when he's right there before us? We drift along, trying our best to muddle through and all the while wondering, "When's God gonna show up?"

He does show up—every day, all day. We just don't recognize him.

For me, God showed up the day I met Father Joseph Kentenich, founder of The Apostolic Movement of Schoenstatt, an international Catholic lay movement of moral and religious renewal. When I was just a year old, my mother and I visited Father Kentenich at the home of a neighbor. There he blessed me and dedicated me to the Blessed Virgin Mary. I don't remember a thing about that day, but it was a meeting that has impacted my entire life.

Ever since I learned about this holy priest, I've felt enfolded in his loving fatherliness through his example, wisdom, legacy, and intercession from heaven. I'm convinced that it's been through his inspiration and guidance that I've repeatedly seen God show up in my life.

I began writing down the stories included in this book as a way to savor the times when God showed up in my life. Many of them are about the times when God showed up through the joys and sorrows we've experienced as a family. I've left them frozen in time so you could experience those moments as I did when they occurred.

I've organized the stories by liturgical season, cited related Scripture passages, and added questions for personal reflection or group discussion. Don't read them all at once. Choose one per week (or one every few days, if the Spirit moves you) to enjoy, digest, and share with others. I hope they make you laugh, cry, rejoice, wonder, seek, and meditate. Most importantly, I hope they draw you into a deep, loving relationship with the Blessed Mother and triune God and inspire you to perceive the times that God shows up in your life.

MARGE FENELON

# ADVENT

▮ ▮ ▮ ▮ ▮ ▮ ▮ ▮ ▮ ▮ ▮ ▮ ▮ ▮ ▮ ▮ ▮ ▮ ▮ ▮ ▮ ▮ ▮ ▮ ▮ ▮ ▮ ▮ ▮ ▮ ▮ ▮ ▮

## Snapshots

"HEY, MOM!" Matt called. "Can you come up here for a minute?"

"Oh, great," I thought. "Now what broke?" Two boys alone upstairs together, and now they were summoning me to the scene of the crime. I tried to be courageous as I mounted the stairs. John, age four, trailed along behind me so as not to miss the excitement.

I found fifteen-year-old Matt and nine-year-old Luke in my bedroom, sitting on my bed. Everything looked to be in relatively good order, except that they had cleared everything off my old memory chest. My memory chest is an old military footlocker that belonged to my husband's uncle during his service in World War II. Now it's filled with snapshots, certificates, medals, newspaper clippings, and other memorabilia from both Mark's family and mine.

"Do you mind if we look at the stuff in here?" Matt asked. "We promise not to wreck anything."

They must have sensed my hesitation, because they both looked at me with their best-honest-to-goodness faces.

"Okay," I said hesitantly, "but be very, very careful. Lay everything in neat piles, and don't finger any of the pictures or you'll ruin them."

"Mom, we pro-o-mise," Matt assured me.

I stood for a minute or two, watching over them. I wanted to make sure they'd hold good on their promise. But before I knew it, I was sit-

1

ting on the bed, too, sifting through snapshots and portraits, fingering old medals, and re-reading old newspaper articles.

We dug our way through more than a hundred years of family history. Every so often, I stopped to linger over a photo or trinket. As I did so, I told the boys the stories I had learned as a girl about relatives of long ago. Often, I knew the story from first-hand experience and would revel in its memory. They soaked it all in, laughing at antics of the past, awed at honors won, sad over losses suffered. The four of us sat there for what seemed like a minute or two but had actually been a few hours. We laid the last snapshot on the pile and began to clean up. I heaved a sigh of disappointment. I wanted the trunk to be like the widow's oil jar—never empty.

I thought of all those faces from the past and yearned for them. I wanted them to come alive again for myself and for my children. The people in the snapshots looked up with expression-filled faces as if they were quite aware that we were gazing back down at them. But they weren't. They had no idea that a misty-eyed mom and her three curious boys were peeking into their little world. They knew only the present—the never-changing eternal present confined by the film.

It's fitting that we rambled through my memory trunk at Advent time, because there is an interesting parallel. Snapshots and Advent. They have much in common, because just as the people in the photos pause in their eternal present, the Christ Child pauses in his eternal present. The tiny Child of long ago is still the tiny Child of today. He waits for us to gaze into his blessed eyes, just as the people in the snapshots wait for us to gaze into theirs. Advent comes every single year, and every single year the holy Child waits for us to come and find him. He is there, constantly, vigilantly, and unceasingly.

Oh, we may change; we *do* change significantly from year to year. We grow, mature, become a bit grayer, take on new responsibilities, deepen our faith, make new friends, and strengthen our relationships with old friends. Our possessions change; our surroundings change. We are different people as we enter each new Advent.

But our Savior doesn't change. He will forever be the same magnificent, loving, glorious little Child who came to earth in order to redeem us. He is there, every single Advent, without fail. He is the omnipotent, omni-present Lord of all. He is the Alpha and the Omega. He is the one true God. He is the Word Incarnate.

However, there is an important difference between snapshots and Advent. The difference is that the people in the photos aren't aware of our presence, but little Jesus is very much aware that we are here. He summons us from the manger. He waits for us in the quiet of the winter night. He radiates his love through the star of Bethlehem. He welcomes us through the faces of his holy mother and foster father. He calls to us in the hymns of old. He draws us closer and closer as we prepare for his birth. He is the eternal present whom we find anew through our Advent longing.

If you have some family snapshots, bring them out this Advent. Gaze into the faces of the people from the past. Think about their eternal present. Thank God for the important part they have played, and still do play, in your life. Then think about the eternal present of the Christ Child. Gaze into his holy face. Revel in his love for you. Bask in your longing for him. Thank him for the important part he has played and still does play in your life.

## What does Scripture say?

*And we know that the Son of God has come and has given us understanding so that we may know him who is true; and we are in him who is true, in his Son Jesus Christ. He is the true God and eternal life.*

1 JOHN 5:20

## What does my heart say?

**|** Who are the people who have the greatest impact on my life?
**|** How can I allow Jesus to have greater impact on my life through them?
**|** How can I allow Jesus to have greater impact on others through me?

∎ ∎ ∎ ∎
# Shepherd for a Day

I WAS SITTING in the pew in the middle of our parish church, immersed in the quiet of eucharistic adoration. I was focused on the gleaming, golden monstrance with the host delicately framed within its beauty, when I heard from behind me a noise that I couldn't identify. "Shuffle-tap, shuffle-tap, shuffle-tap." It was slowly making its way up the center aisle.

*Must be a disabled person with a cane or an elderly person with a walker,* I said to myself. Curious, I watched out of the corner of my eye to see this dedicated person who refused to let a physical impediment stop him or her from paying tribute to the King. "Shuffle-tap, shuffle-tap." It was coming closer—right next to me now.

What I saw amazed me. It was not a disabled person at all, but a poor, thin, middle-aged Hispanic man. Dressed in plain working-man clothes, hat in hand, head bowed, he was walking on his knees up the center aisle toward the altar. "Shuffle-tap, shuffle-tap." I felt myself barely breathing as my eyes followed him and I anticipated what he was going to do next. His absolute humility awed me.

Slowly he journeyed to the front of the church, never looking up for so much as an instant. Once there, he paused, motionless, still on his knees, with his head hung. He prayed there, in front of the Blessed Sacrament, for a long time. When he had finished, he meekly tipped his head up, rose, walked to the side aisle, and left the church. I sat there for another half hour, contemplating what I'd observed.

This man, with his reverence and simplicity, reminded me of the shepherds in Bethlehem who left their fields to pay tribute to the King. They were not dignitaries or wealthy merchants. Certainly they were not highly educated—I doubt they were even educated at all. They were of the unpretentious working class who had to labor endlessly to scrape together a living for themselves, just as I suppose this man did. Yet the angels appeared to them, inviting them to be the first outside of the Holy Family to experience the mystery of the Incarnation. I wondered if the same angels could have called *this* man to experience the mystery of the Incarnation.

What impressed me most about this man's manner was the way it reflected his relationship with Jesus. He certainly wasn't there for appearances, for he never once looked up to see if anyone was looking back. He was there to visit his Christ, to pay him homage in the most profound way in which he was capable. He had set aside the worries and obligations of the world in order to seek out the desire of his heart. Perhaps he had just come from work or was on his way to work. Perhaps he was about to go to an appointment or run some errands. Whatever the case, he left his usual activity in order to honor Jesus. Just like the shepherds.

I wish I could be a shepherd for a day. I think it would be great to be able to live in such an unassuming way. No telephones. No doorbells. No televisions. No emails. No deadlines. No meetings. I'd have just a few meager possessions and a bunch of bleating, fuzzy mammals to keep me company. Then I'd be able to drop everything, just like the shepherds, in order to seek out and pay tribute to the King.

Advent is upon us, and it's got me thinking a whole lot more seriously about this shepherd thing. I've even been eyeing the striped broadcloth at the fabric store. The other day, I caught myself scanning the nature CDs at the discount store to see if I could find one that had sheep noises. I find the idea of wearing one of those head coverings a rather appealing remedy for a bad hair day. And I've always been a sandal person. Of course, with four energetic kids, a rambunctious dog, and a hyper guinea pig, I could find many uses for one of those staffs.

All right, all right. I realize this change of identity is really just a dream. (Or a nightmare for my kids who want to invite their friends over to the house. "Come on in. This is my…uh…mom. She…really… ummm…watches over us." "Hello Mrs. Fenelon. Nice…uh…hat.") But to keep my own identity and live the shepherd mentality throughout Advent might be more doable.

The man at my parish church had the shepherd attitude I desire for myself. He didn't put on any airs. He wasn't worried about what he had or didn't have. He didn't care about what others might think of him. He was there for one purpose only. He approached the Almighty slowly, determinedly, and reverently. He offered the King the best he could—his plain, old, loving self in body, mind, and spirit. He put aside all else in order to pay tribute to the King.

## What does Scripture say?

> *In that region there were shepherds living in the fields, keeping watch over their flock by night. Then an angel of the Lord stood before them, and the glory of the Lord shone around them, and they were terrified. But the angel said to them, "Do not be afraid; for see—I am bringing you good news of great joy for all the people: to you is born this day in the city of David a Savior, who is the Messiah, the Lord. This will be a sign for you: you will find a child wrapped in bands of cloth and lying in a manger."*
>
> LUKE 2:8–12

## What does my heart say?

**I** What is the field I must leave in order to pay tribute to the King?

**I** What does the mystery of the Incarnation mean to me?

**I** What is the most profound way that I can pay homage to Christ?

■ ▌ ■

# One Big Baby

JESUS MUST HAVE BEEN one BIG baby. At least that's what my daughter thinks. At four years of age, Monica takes the term "big and strong" literally. She thinks parents can do anything because they're "big and strong." Men can do more than women because they're bigger and stronger. In her eyes, any person or thing of measurable size is stronger, smarter, and more qualified.

In that case, Jesus must be absolutely huge, because he's able to keep her safe from anything. Likely, she thinks that our Lord was raised on nothing but wheat germ and broccoli—and all those other foods she's been told to eat because they'll make her grow big and strong. She probably sees Jesus as a towering figure who rises above the rooftops—a sort of invisible giant who wanders around looking for good deeds to perform. I can't imagine how her little mind pictures the lowly stable in Bethlehem!

Because of this, Monica is fairly fearless. Being in her room alone at night never bothers her. Waiting outside the door for Mommy to use the bathroom is a piece of cake. Seeing something scurry away in the grass is no problem. No creature, great or small, furry or slimy, intimidates her. She's the one (much to the chagrin of her older brother) who charges into the dark basement yelling, "It's okay, Mom. I don't care about the dark or the spiders. Jesus will keep me safe."

Oh, to have the faith of a child! Wouldn't if be nice if we adults could throw ourselves into the darkness calling behind us, "It's okay. I don't care about the dark. Jesus will keep me safe"?

Stop and watch the children around you during this Advent. We have so much to learn from them. They so readily accept the Advent message. They wait, although none too patiently, for the birth of Jesus and all the magic that includes. They work studiously at being good for the coming of Santa Claus, Kris Kringle, the Magi, the Christ Child, or whoever brings gifts to their family at Christmas. They dream of the presents they'll receive, of the fleets of angels and the gentle shepherds. They wonder at the stillness of the Holy Night when a tiny (or not so tiny, in my daughter's estimation) baby came to bring goodness and salvation to the world. They ponder the enchantment of the Epiphany and the lure of the star of Bethlehem. They wait and dream and ponder, but mostly they wait.

They wait but never doubt. They know that when the calendar turns to December, it's time for surprises and excitement. They trust that on Christmas morning, their fondest wishes will be fulfilled. And although they may not be able to understand the full impact of Jesus' birth, they believe with their whole hearts that it means something wonderful for all of mankind.

We adults also believe and wait, but seldom do it in childlike confidence. We let our skepticism get in the way. We let doubts creep in. We lose the ability to wonder as a child does—to accept this great gift of a Savior in the very depths of our hearts.

Meditate on the children. Savor their innocence and enthusiasm. Make their carefree attitude your own. Let the cards sit for a while. Put away the wrapping paper. Say "no" to a few of those parties. Read the story of the Nativity from a children's book and revel in its simplicity. Say the rosary and meditate on the Joyful Mysteries. Or, just spend some time sitting in silence. Count the gifts that the Christ Child has to offer you. Become a spiritual child and let your heart absorb the message of Advent.

Monica was right. Jesus *IS* one big baby, in terms of his strength, wisdom, and love. He can keep us safe from anything. If we rely on his strength, we'll be able to accomplish everything the heavenly Father wills for us. If we seek his wisdom, he will guide us in every circumstance, no matter how painful or perplexing it may be. And if we immerse ourselves in the ocean of his loving mercy, our hearts will find peace and contentment even when our adult world seems to come crashing in on us. With childlike confidence, we'll be able to leap into the dark because we know that Jesus will keep us safe.

## What does Scripture say?

*People were bringing little children to him in order that he might touch them; and the disciples spoke sternly to them. But when Jesus saw this, he was indignant and said to them, "Let the little children come to me; do not stop them; for it is to such as these that the kingdom of God belongs. Truly I tell you, whoever does not receive the kingdom of God as a little child will never enter it." And he took them up in his arms, laid his hands on them, and blessed them.*

MARK 10:13–16

## What does my heart say?

- **I** What inhibitions, selfish ambitions and unrealistic expectations must I let go of before I'm able to open my heart to the Christ Child?
- **I** How can I increase my trust in Jesus to the point that I'm able to leap into the dark?
- **I** What does my darkness look like?

■ I I ■
# What Will Become of This Child?

ONE EVENING, as I sat reading a Bible story to my children, six-year-old Matthew stopped me cold in order to ask one of his famous too-big-for-your-britches theological questions.

"Mom, did Jesus know he was God even when he was a baby? Because, if he did, then he should have known how to eat and walk and talk and stuff already, because God knows everything!"

What's a mother to do? I did the only thing I *could* do, the only thing any good mother would do when faced with such an intriguing question ten minutes before bedtime. I said, "I don't know."

Call it mother's intuition, but there was something about his hurricane-gust sigh and the rolling of his eyes that told me he wasn't exactly satisfied with that answer. I could tell I wasn't about to get away with it this time.

We've probably all thought about this question sometime in our lives and, after some confusion, just sort of filed it away with all the other questions that are too deep or difficult or abstract. Did Jesus' enlightenment concerning his true identity come gradually? Could it be possible that his first real taste of his destiny was when Mary and Joseph found him conversing with the teachers in the Temple? Or could it have been that Jesus was indeed aware of his power from the moment of birth, but chose to keep his identity hidden until the proper time? He clearly knew by the time he attended the marriage feast at Cana.

With our limited human intellects and experiences, we could imagine that, as Jesus approached the age of reason, God sat down with him for a heavenly Father-to-Son talk. Poor little Jesus. Maybe he went running home to the Blessed Mother crying, "Mother, do you know what he told me? He told me I'm God!" And the Blessed Mother would have smiled and said, "Well, Son, I've been meaning to tell you..."

Of course, we all know that my imagined version is far from the truth. As Father John Hardon states in his catechism, "Jesus knew from the moment of his conception that he was divine. To suppose that his human soul only gradually came to know he was divine would be to deny that he was true God and true man from the first instant of the Incarnation in his mother's womb" (*The Question and Answer Catholic Catechism*).

How difficult it is to comprehend this mystery, to think that the Almighty God took the form of a mere child, just like the children we have in our lives—the same creatures for whom we mend skinned knees, wash dirty faces, and teach to walk, talk, and feed themselves. And then to go a step further and realize that, at the very moment he was learning to walk, talk, eat, and was having his skinned knees mended and dirty face washed, he retained the awareness and power of his divine nature.

No matter how we imagine Jesus' life on earth, the fact remains that God sent his only Son to redeem us. The Redeemer, both as God and Man, knew well the same trials and tribulations that we humans face in trying to discover and carry out the mission that God has for each one of us. While Jesus' wisdom and power far outweigh our own, there is one thing that we do have in common. We also came to earth as helpless infants and must realize our true identity and the implications that has for the world around us.

Finding the path God has laid for us is tricky. If you're like me, you spend most of your time bumping into brick walls until you've taken three quarters of the skin off your nose and a little off each cheek as well. After that, if you're lucky, you realize you're heading in the wrong direction. Some of us are fortunate enough to learn after the first scrape or two.

But for all of us, it's a growing process. Little by little we absorb the information God has for us. We hear it in the silences of holy places. We hear it in the voices of others. We hear it in the stillness of our hearts. We hear it in a job well done, or an inspiring experience. And we hear it in our painful mistakes and misunderstandings.

Unlike our Savior who knew from the beginning, it may take years for us to get the gist of what God is trying to tell us. Thankfully, we have a merciful Father in Heaven who is willing to wait patiently for us to find our way. We have a loving Blessed Mother who is always ready to mend our skinned knees and wash our dirty faces. Sometimes even we adults need to take baby steps for a while. We're never as wise as we think we are. Nor, I think, do we ever finish growing up. As children of God, we'll spend our whole lives learning "to eat and walk and talk and stuff."

## What does Scripture say?

> *For you did not receive a spirit of slavery to fall back into fear, but you have received a spirit of adoption. When we cry, "Abba! Father!" it is that very Spirit bearing witness with our spirit that we are children of God, and if children, then heirs, heirs of God and joint heirs with Christ—if, in fact, we suffer with him so that we may also be glorified with him.*
>
> ROMANS 8:15–17

## What does my heart say?

▌ Somewhere deep inside each of us, there is a little child. What kind of child is inside of me?

▌ How is my child growing?

▌ What does my child do when he or she encounters the unknown?

# CHRISTMAS

## Why THIS Place?

I CAN'T UNDERSTAND what she saw in this place. When we decided that it was time to move, we prayed fervently to the Blessed Mother, asking her to find a new house for us. We made little paper crowns and glued paper jewels to them, each "jewel" representing a personal sacrifice we had made. We promised Mary a formal coronation once we were settled into our new home. We wanted the choice to be hers. Whatever house she chose would be her dwelling place, her throne, and we would be happy to live there with her.

But here? This isn't at all what I had imagined.

"Ask and you shall receive," Jesus said. We received, but I'm just not sure what it is we've received. This place, from the barren scratched-up floors to the kicked-in walls and doors, to the woodwork with obscene death threats carved into it, is the ultimate handyman special. There's barely a spot in the entire house that isn't in need of some kind of repair.

On each of our visits to view the house before we made the offer to purchase, the furniture had been strategically placed so as to hide the flaws. We knew there'd be plenty of fixing up to do, but we had no idea of the full extent of the damage. Even the inspector we hired missed the lion's share of the repairs and renovations that would be required to make the house habitable.

The worst part is not that we have to fix all the damage, but that it was caused by the previous owners out of vengeance toward us and anger toward each other. Our real estate deal with them turned sour, and we were forced to pursue a legal battle just two weeks before closing. That's when the demolition crew set to work, the neighbors say. But they also told us that this was a truly troubled family, long before we entered the picture. I believe it.

As Mark and I, along with many self-sacrificing friends and family members, cleaned away the filth and rubbish those first weeks, I could feel the deep sadness of this other family. It was as if I could place my ear to the walls and hear them sobbing; my fingertips could feel the vibrations of their fury. There were several heavy-duty locks on bedroom doors. What made them so fearful? Sections of wallpaper were torn down. What made them so agitated? Windows were broken. What was behind their rage? Paint-chipped woodwork was everywhere. What had caused them so much pain?

There are so many families like this in our society: the family in the inner city so overwrought with hopelessness that they turn to violence; the suburban family whose career-driven parents begin to hate each other; the middle class family torn by alcoholism due to job loss; spouses who change partners as easily as they change their socks.

Families become like the one that moved out of our house because they lack a spiritual home, a refuge from the confusion of the world. They have no prayer life, no membership in a faith community, no respect for family relationships, and no center.

I feel guilty admitting that I hesitated setting up our prayer corner, or home shrine, to the Blessed Virgin Mary when we first moved in. In fact, I waited more than a week. Why? I'm not sure. I think I felt as if this was no place for her to be—an unfit spot for her to erect her throne. I wanted something marvelous and had only something tattered to offer.

When I finally did put it up, I cringed at the thought of mounting her beautiful picture against these ugly walls. Yet I knew we'd be as lost as the family before us without her. They were a family with a house, but not a home.

What a vast contrast to the Holy Family! They had a home, but not a house. Forced to travel to far-away Bethlehem for the census, they were denied even the most basic of comforts. Mary had to give birth to our Savior in a pile of hay instead of a birthing bed. Saint Joseph had no cushy armchair in which to rest and hold his newborn son. Gleeful relatives did not surround them; they announced the birth to a bunch of stable animals. And yet, they did not lack a home.

They were at home in God's love. United in the joy of following his holy will, they were at peace. Their surroundings didn't matter. What mattered was what lay inside their hearts. Their security was divine, not temporal.

Someday this house will be beautiful—with a ton of patience and elbow grease. But because we so love God and each other, as the Holy Family did, it is already a home.

## What does Scripture say?

*While they were there, the time came for her to deliver her child. And she gave birth to her firstborn son and wrapped him in bands of cloth, and laid him in a manger, because there was no place for them in the inn.*

LUKE 2:6–7

## What does my heart say?

∎ When have I ever felt "at home" in God's love?
∎ What made me feel that way?
∎ How can I re-create that feeling in a very practical way?

∎ ∎ ∎ ∎
# A Child's Love

NO DOUBT ABOUT IT: John truly, deeply loves me. I can see it, and anybody around me can see it, too. His love bubbles out of him like one of those bubble-blowing horns you can buy at the discount store. It "blurbbles" and "blabbles" all over the place. Hundreds of times a day, it seems, he puts down whatever it is he's gotten his four-year-old hands into, searches me out, and tells me how much he loves me. "Big as the world. No, bigger than the world," he says. Then he proceeds to squeeze me until both of our faces are red. We don't really need a radio or CD player around our house. Just about any time of the day you'll hear John singing, "I love Mommy and Daddy" to the melodies of Mozart, Haydn, or Beethoven. And of course, there are few mornings I wake up without his hot little breath gracing my face.

John is especially demonstrative of his affection during Mass. His favorite thing to do is to fling his rounded little arms around me and give me minute-long sequences of big, smoochy kisses. LOUD, big, smoochy kisses, the kind that makes people turn around in order to find the source.

If I weren't such a glutton for a child's love, I would curb that Mass-time habit so as not to disturb the other folks who are trying to pray. I would gently set him down next to me and explain that church isn't the right place for smoochy kisses. I would tell him that we could do smoochy kisses while we're at home, snuggling together on the couch over a story. Then I would draw his attention to the altar where the priest is preparing the bread and wine, or perhaps to one of the many saint statues. That's what I *should* do, but not what I actually do.

Instead I revel in his love, soaking it up as if I were a giant sponge. I try to memorize every squinty-eyed smile and pucker, every squeak in his voice, and the softness of his skin. I cling to these moments, because I know that one day he'll be too grown up for smoochy kisses. And then I'll miss them dearly.

Young children are so free with their love; they haven't yet learned the stuffiness of adults. They aren't worried about making a scene when they climb up on their daddies' shoulders or throw kisses to their mommies. They aren't afraid to proclaim their love in public. When they give their love, they don't wait around expecting something in return. They give it because they instinctively know that love is something to be given away unconditionally.

As I sit with John wormed tightly into my lap, I like to contemplate the love between the Blessed Mother and our Lord. What was the moment like when the she beheld her son for the first time? She knew he was the Savior and at the same time, he was a part of her own flesh. Hidden away from the rest of the world in a dusky, meager stable, she literally saw the face of God, and that face gazed back at her with love. Had Jesus done "puppy-nuggles" in Mary's arms when he was young? Had he flung his beautiful little arms around her and smothered her in big, smoochy kisses? Did he ever sing the "I Love You" song to her?

I can imagine that the Child Jesus certainly did sing the "I Love You" song to the Blessed Mother, although in that time and place, the words and music would have been quite different. But I can also imagine that the Child Jesus sang the "I Love You" song to each and every one of us. How pleased he must have been to finally be among us, to begin his tremendous mission here on earth. He had come to redeem the world, and his entire life and death would become one great "I Love You" song. Instead of big, smoochy kisses and "puppy-nuggles," he'd come to smother us in his love and mercy.

## What does Scripture say?

*When the angels had left them and gone into heaven, the shepherds said to one another, "Let us go now to Bethlehem and see this thing that has taken place, which the Lord has made known to us." So they went with haste and found Mary and Joseph, and the child lying in the manger. When they saw this, they made known what had been told them about this child; and all who heard it were amazed at what the shepherds told them. But Mary treasured all these words and pondered them in her heart.*

LUKE 2:15–19

## What does my heart say?

▎ Can I pinpoint times when Jesus has smothered me in big, smoochy kisses and "puppy-nuggles"?

▎ How do I accept that love?

▎ How do I return that love?

 **LENT**

■ ▎ ▎ ▎ ■ ▎ ▎ ▎ ■ ▎ ▎ ▎ ■ ▎ ▎ ▎ ■ ▎ ▎ ▎ ■ ▎ ▎ ▎ ■ ▎ ▎ ▎ ■

## Multi-colored Madonna

I COULD HEAR the voices escalating in the other room.

"Now what?" I asked myself. I put down my mixing spoon and went by the doorway to listen. Child psychologists say parents should let siblings fight their own battles, and that they learn to resolve conflicts more efficiently that way. But I've never been able to completely ignore the ruckus.

Normally, the squabble stops as soon as they figure out that Mom's not going to take sides. This time was different. It wasn't your typical you'd-better-quit-bugging-me fight. The roar was turning into a sonic boom. Worse, the one yelling the loudest was our five-year old Monica. *Monica?* Impossible! Not the little girl we nicknamed "Princess" because of her royal mannerisms and graciousness!

"This ought to be good," I said to myself as I moved into a more strategic spying location.

"Monica, you can't color the Blessed Mother all different colors like that!" screamed eight-year-old Matthew.

"Yes, I can!" sobbed Monica.

"Uh-uh!" Matthew shot back. "You're supposed to make her face peach and her veil blue. That's the way it is in all the pictures."

"But Mom said I can color my coloring books any way I want to!" Monica stomped her foot on the floor.

Terrific. Now I'd been dragged into it. I was forced to come out of my hiding place and face the consequences of my folly.

"Mom, didn't you say I could color in my coloring book any way I want to?" Monica begged with great crystal tears streaming down her face.

I had. And at that moment, I wished I hadn't. In fact, I regretted everything I had ever taught my kids about individuality. I took the book from Monica's trembling little hand. I had to admit; the Madonna did look a bit peculiar with her face striped with fuchsia, brown, crimson, frog green, and a variety of other indescribable colors.

"Mom, you told us we have to respect holy things," prodded Matthew. "Isn't it disrespectful to make the Blessed Mother's face all goofy like that?"

"It isn't goofy! She looks pretty that way!" insisted Monica. I knew I wasn't going to get out of this one easily. Unfortunately, they were both right. We need to respect holy things *and* Monica can color in her coloring book anyway she wants to. After calling a cease-fire and imposing a truce, I went back to my bread dough.

I had to smile to myself as I thought about the war zone I'd just vacated. The children certainly had learned to stick up for their individual convictions. That's a quality Mark and I try hard to foster in us and inspire in our children.

That isn't easy to do these days. In a world in which we're all expected to follow the latest trends, those who color their world a little differently are ostracized. We're working on teaching our kids to color their worlds according to God's palette, not according to the culture.

I spent some time contemplating Monica's response to Matthew's chiding. She was determined to color the Blessed Mother in the way she felt called; rainbow striping gave her tribute, not insult. If she wanted a multi-colored Madonna, she should be able to have one.

We all must do the same. She's the Mother of God, and also our mother. The heavenly Father wills that we venerate and imitate her, even if it's not the culturally popular thing to do. It's as if he's presented each of us with a blank coloring page and asks us to color her image in the way we are uniquely called. For some of us, that means multi-colored striping; for others, it means a peach face and blue veil. Or, it could mean something entirely different. In any case, we must keep our palette before us and make a life long commitment to finish the portrait.

Now is an especially good time to work on our pictures. Lent is traditionally the time to focus on the sufferings of Christ, and rightfully so. However, we mustn't forget the anguish that the Blessed Mother experienced as she watched him tortured and die a gruesome death. In spite of the torment she felt inside, she remained strong and silent, because she knew that unless the Father's will was fulfilled, we would have no recourse to heaven. It's her total surrender to the triune God that we're called to imitate, and we must do that by drawing from our own individual palettes of gifts, abilities, and tendencies—even if that means making her a multi-colored Madonna.

## What does Scripture say?

*And that is what the soldiers did. Meanwhile, standing near the cross of Jesus were his mother, and his mother's sister, Mary the wife of Clopas, and Mary Magdalene.*

JOHN 19:25

## What does my heart say?

∎ What does the palette of my own talents, skill, strengths and weaknesses look like?
∎ What does my picture of the Blessed Mother look like thus far in my life?
∎ How can I refine it?

■  I  I  ■

# Speed and Spirituality

GOD TOOK AWAY my speedometer the other day. I was rounding a curve on the highway and it began buzzing and bouncing all over the place like a kid who's eaten an entire chocolate cake all by himself. It's the only time in my life I've gone from 40 to 120 in a split second without having had a second cup of morning coffee. Impressive. The most amazing thing is that the trees still seemed to be taking their good-natured time passing me by. That's when I knew for certain that my speedometer had kicked the bucket, because trees never take their good-natured time passing me by when I'm behind the wheel.

Of course, this posed an interesting problem. I had to rely on others to judge how fast I was going, and that's not a very comfortable feeling. One way I found was to choose the most conscientious looking driver on the road and keep apace of him or her. Not only was that boring, but with the proliferation of folks doing any number of unusual things while driving, it was a rarity. Imagine my frustration when there were no other cars on the road. Thinking I was flying along at top speed, I'd be overtaken by a vicious pack of cars heartlessly passing me by and leaving me in the dust. Sometimes, if I was savvy enough, I could gun it and coast along on their tailwind. Other times, I had the great fortune of getting a feel for the road and clipping along so as to gain on a pack and watch it minimize in the rear view mirror. But the snicker melted off my face pretty quickly as I glided up behind the next pack of cars that were all jammed into a cloister because there was a cop cozied up behind the bridge pilings. A good friend of mine suggested that I watch for drivers with one of those marvelous little black boxes on their dashboards, but I never spotted one. When your speedometer keels over, you're at the mercy of the world around you.

It intrigues me that this incident occurred at the approach of Lent—the time to delve deeply into the gadgets and gizmos of what makes me tick and evaluate where I am in my spiritual formation. I often find myself attempting to manage my spiritual life in much the same way that I attempted to drive with a faulty speedometer. When I see people way ahead of me spiritually, I try to race ahead to catch up with them, placing more and more demands on myself hoping that I'll get caught up in their tailwind. In the end, I have to slam on the brakes because the heavenly Father sends a traffic jam warning me that I'm moving too fast. On the other hand, there are times when I'm drifting totally on my own and I think I'm developing at a good pace, only to be side-swiped by one of his messengers who's *really* clipping along. Then I realize that all I've been doing is puttering along without really getting anywhere. At other times, I find myself trying to merge into the spirituality of those who tend to cloister together, pumping the brakes so as not to take on too much. This only makes me miserable because I feel stifled and tethered. Regardless of the speed, if it's someone else's, then it's not right for me.

In order to find my personal "mph," I have to put aside my own selfish laziness, desires, and fears and pay careful attention to the needles and gauges that God has placed before me in my life. He is the ultimate speedometer. With gentle signals, he lovingly controls my speed through the sacraments, the Scriptures, my spiritual exercises, and my spiritual director. He speeds me up through the various good works that call upon me to meet the needs of others. He scoops me up in the tailwinds of world events. He hums me along through my husband, my children, and the way we work together as a family and through the thousands of little occurrences that happen each day. He slows me down in the depth and quietude of my heart as I meditate on my spiritual resolutions and personal mission. He brings me to an idle when my soul cries out for peace and nourishment in the solace of the Blessed Sacrament and in the comfort of his holy Mother.

As I travel on my long journey through Lent, I realize that I'm actually grateful that my speedometer went on the blink, even though it cost me a bundle to replace. It was a sharp reminder that my focus needs to be on my internal spiritual speedometer and not on the progress of the rest of the vehicles on the road. By maintaining the speed that the heavenly Father has designated for me, I'll indeed become a useful vehicle for him on the highway of his divine plan.

## What does Scripture say?

*We do not dare to classify or compare ourselves with some of those who commend themselves. But when they measure themselves by one another, and compare themselves with one another, they do not show good sense.*

2 CORINTHIANS 10:12

## What does my heart say?

- **I** How do I know when my spiritual speedometer is working?
- **I** Who do I most often compare myself to: those I perceive to be ahead of me or those who are behind me?
- **I** What does this tell me about the way I perceive my own spirituality?

∎ ∎ ∎ ∎
# The Banana Man

I HAD TO DO the grocery shopping alone one hectic Saturday morning. Usually, I haul one of the kids along for the sake of having company, but also to help with the packing and carrying. No one was available this time. I dislike crowds and especially crowded grocery stores and so going alone was simply out of the question. Realizing that no good mother could refuse the request of a desperate child, I asked the Blessed Mother to spiritually accompany me. I promised not to make her pack and carry anything and hoped she'd agree.

As I moved through the aisles, I struck up a mental conversation between Mary and myself. It was the kind of self-talk that other folks might find alarming if I were expressing myself aloud. We delved into a lively discussion about what I'm capable of handling on my own and what things are simply out of my control. I'm afraid I was discovering more of the latter than the former. Sometimes it can be downright exasperating to look at where I am now and where I'd like to be on my spiritual journey! Nevertheless, the Blessed Mother and I were happy as larks, conversing together and not paying much attention to what was going on around us. At least *I* wasn't.

Before long, I found myself in the produce aisle, standing in front of the banana crates. I began to reach for a bag of bananas, when suddenly I heard a deep, kind voice from right behind me, practically in my ear.

"Here, let me reach the good ones in the back for you," said the voice. "I have longer arms than you do."

As I turned around, I was touched and amazed. There stood a lively yet elderly man with a pleasant smile and gentle manner. He leaned over and pulled a bag of bananas from one of the back crates. After he handed me the first one, I apologetically asked for another.

"How many would you like?" he asked patiently.

"Four, please," I said, a bit embarrassed. Then I explained to him that at our house we go through bananas like water, because we use them to make fruit smoothies for breakfast almost every morning.

"That's a great idea," he said without a flinch. "There, is that enough?" he asked, handing me the fourth bag.

"Yes. Thank you," I responded. Then before he went on his way, I added, "That was a very kind gesture, and I appreciate it very much."

"You're welcome," he said as he disappeared into the crowd.

As I finished my shopping, I marveled at the man's thoughtfulness. He was there to help without my even having expressed a need for it. Truly, I wasn't even aware of his presence until he had spoken.

Are there times in our lives when we feel as though we're standing at the banana crates, unable to reach the unblemished ones in the back? It's at those moments when we see the discrepancy between what we think we can handle on our own and what is simply out of our control—when the ideal and the reality don't coincide—that we can feel discouraged enough to give up.

Original sin prohibits us from becoming perfect. But we have a special partner on our spiritual journey who mediates the grace and strength we need to slowly, step by step, continue the arduous journey toward the highest ideals. Jesus gave us this partner when he hung on the cross.

"When Jesus saw his mother and the disciple whom he loved standing beside her, he said to his mother, 'Woman, here is your son.' Then he said to the disciple, 'Here is your mother.' And from that hour the disciple took her into his own home" (John 19:26–27).

Jesus' dying words confirmed Mary's motherhood of all humankind and guarantees that she will be at our side always, no matter how far in the distance the ideal looms or how hard reality hits us. She gives us the perfect example of the child who constantly seeks the Father's will, even in the most difficult moments. As all good mothers lead their children to their father, the Blessed Mother leads us to our heavenly Father, and through her we are drawn into his merciful love.

When we stand at the edge of the chasm—lost in our own weaknesses, anxieties, confusion, and shortcomings—he's there in his merciful love to help us before we even express the need. When we're reaching as far as we can for the ideal and still coming up short, he shows up behind us and tells us, "I have longer arms than you do." And sometimes we weren't even aware of his presence until he had spoken.

## What does Scripture say?

*The LORD is gracious and merciful,*
*slow to anger and abounding in steadfast love.*

PSALM 145:8

## What does my heart say?

∎ When have I felt as though I were standing at the banana crates?
∎ How did the merciful Father's arms reach where I could not?
∎ What are the "blemished bananas" that most affect me now?

■ I I ■

# Unexpected Evangelization

I HAVE a confession to make. I'm a terrible evangelist, at least face-to-face. Put me in front of a keyboard, and I have no trouble turning out pages and pages about the wonder and beauty of the Catholic Church. Put me in front of another human being without a chance to prepare beforehand and I stutter and falter until my tongue is tied in knots.

That's why I can't understand how, on a summer night in a Milwaukee hospital room, God chose me to defend the credibility of the Church to a young nurse searching to regain her faith.

I was hospitalized for a short time that July after having contracted a serious systemic infection. While I was feeling under the weather, I wasn't too sick to strike up a conversation (several of them, actually) with my second-shift nurse. We had a lot in common and hit if off right from the start. Usually the topics were light and general.

One of the last nights of my stay, we were hee-hawing over something crazy we'd heard on the news, when out of the blue, she asked me where I get my faith.

I was stunned. Where in the world had that question come from? The only outward sign of my spirituality was a small copy of my favorite image of Mary as Mother Thrice Admirable, Queen and Victress of Schoenstatt. I'd hung it on the bulletin board in my room to keep me company. It's not as if I had brought an altar and tabernacle with me!

Regardless of the question's origin, the nurse had placed it before me and was waiting anxiously for an answer. What was I supposed to tell her? My faith is the culmination of decades of influence by other people, circumstances, and education. Most importantly, my faith is a gift from God. Without a keyboard or even so much as a scratch pad and pencil to fall back on, I tried my best to explain to her how I came to know and love the Church.

Before long, the nurse was tearfully telling me about her own experiences with the Church. She told me about her alcoholic father and the way her mother desperately tried to shield the family's four children from her father's vengeance. She told me about her disillusionment with the Church after having seen her mother, a devout Catholic, pray ceaselessly for years seemingly without results. She told me about how all the traditions and customs of the Church—the things most of us hold so dear—came to disgust her. Worse, she told me about the emptiness she felt and her sorrow for her three young children. Because of her self-alienation from the Church, she said, her children have no faith life.

I wish I could say that I wisely counseled her. I wish I could say that I helped her to get her faith life back in order and opened her eyes once again to the glory of the Holy Catholic Church. But I didn't. Frankly, I didn't know what to say, so I said nothing and just listened. I couldn't even hug her because of the way I was hooked up to the IVs.

Instead, I ended up talking in generalizations about why people leave the Church and why some come back and some don't. I told her why I knew I could never, ever leave the Church.

To my relief, she was called over the intercom to go to another room. My relief soon turned into disappointment—in myself. Why hadn't I said something profound? Why hadn't I invited her to my parish? Why hadn't I asked her to visit one of the Marian shrines in the area with me? Why hadn't I assured her that she'd always be welcomed back into the Church? And why, oh why, had God put me into such a goofy situation?

I never did find the opportunity to tell the nurse the things I'd wished I had. So, I did the next best thing. When I checked out of the hospital, I scribbled a note to her about never giving up her search for her faith. And, I included my picture of the Mother Thrice Admirable—the only tool of evangelization I had to give.

The incident with the hospital nurse made me realize how important it is for all of us to examine the extent of our love for the Church from time to time, especially during Lent. I wonder if we love it enough to openly share it with others, even if we fear becoming tongue-tied. I wonder if we love it enough to commit our lives to it totally. I wonder if we love it enough to die for it, as our Lord and Savior did.

I'll probably never know why God chose that hospital room to ask me to evangelize unexpectedly. I'll probably never forgive myself for being such a coward. I'll probably never find out what happened to that nurse. But I'll continue to pray for her and her family. And, I'll always be grateful that I had the privilege to witness our Mother calling her child back to the Church through something as simple as her picture hanging on a hospital room bulletin board.

### What does Scripture say?

*You are my witnesses, says the LORD,*
*and my servant whom I have chosen,*
*so that you may know and believe me*
*and understand that I am he.*
*Before me no god was formed,*
*nor shall there be any after me.*

ISAIAH 43:10

### What does my heart say?

I When have I been called to a moment of unexpected evangelization?
I What do I like about the way I handled it?
I What would I have liked to do better?

# ▪ ▪ ▪ ▪
# In the Spirit of the Cross

I WAS SITTING in the ophthalmologist's office, waiting to undergo a laser treatment to seal some broken blood vessels near my retina. The procedure, although done frequently by ophthalmologists throughout the country, involved some risks.

As I sat there waiting for the technician to call my name, I felt a cold chill run down my spine, and I began to perspire. I kept thinking about those risks and wondered just what God had in store for me.

I imagined myself getting up, going to the receptionist's desk, and politely telling her, "Thank you kindly, but this just isn't my cup of tea. I'm leaving now." I then pictured myself walking out the door, hopping onto the elevator, and rushing to the safety of my home.

This scenario became so vivid that I actually found myself moving to the edge of my seat. Just at that moment, a smiling young woman in a lab coat called my name. She didn't *look* dangerous. So I followed her.

As we walked together down the corridor, I thought of the imprisonment of Father Joseph Kentenich, founder of The Apostolic Movement of Schoenstatt, by the Gestapo in 1941. In spite of being placed into solitary confinement for four weeks in a dark, airless bank vault, Father Kentenich never wavered in his faith and trust in God's divine providence. Although he could hear the screams and pleadings of the other prisoners as they were interrogated and tortured, he remained steadfast, calm, and completely connected to the Divine. When threatened with imprisonment in the Dachau concentration camp, he peacefully accepted it as God's will.

We entered the treatment room, and the technician strapped my head into the cushioned brace on the seat facing the laser machine. I wondered if my initial impression of her had been faulty. As I waited for the procedure to begin, I thought of the chains and shackles of the prisoners in Dachau. I thought about the ghastly medical experiments performed on some of them in the name of science. Then I thought of

Father Kentenich, waiting in the throes of hopelessness, yet radiating confidence in divine providence.

I felt a bit foolish. There I was, in the hands of a competent physician, undergoing a treatment designed to save my eyesight, and I was acting like a scared puppy. I was so nervous during the procedure that the ophthalmologist had to pause several times to let me regroup before he could continue. The more we paused, the more I thought about the risks and the more nervous I got. By the grace of God, I made it through, and the laser surgery was completely successful. I went home and sat in our prayer corner to say a prayer of thanksgiving. But my thanksgiving was clouded by disappointment in myself. I thought again of Father Kentenich, who had touched the lives of many with his calmness and holiness in the midst of terror and degradation. I thought of all the other holy men and women who had suffered much more than I had for the sake of the Church. Then I thought of the Savior who had shown them the way. We all have such moments in our lives—moments in which we perspire over the risks that we face. We hope that we'll face them with calmness and confidence in divine providence. We may have to pause several times to regroup. We may even fail and become disappointed in ourselves. And that's OK, because it's all part of being human. Even our failures and shortcomings can become sacrifices of love when we offer them to Christ. It's not so much that we immediately attain victory, as that we do everything out of striving in the spirit of the cross.

## What does Scripture say?

*For the message about the cross is foolishness to those who are perishing, but to us who are being saved it is the power of God.*

1 CORINTHIANS 1:18

## What does my heart say?

∎ What is the biggest risk I've ever faced?
∎ How did I face it?
∎ What are some practical ways that will help me to live my life in the spirit of the cross?

■ ∎ ∎ ■
# Slow Down and Live

IT TOOK THE BIRTH of my third child to teach me how to leave the laundry unfolded. As a full-time mom, writer, and workaholic, that was no easy task. It bothers me—um...*bothered* me—to leave things unfinished.

When my first son was just a baby, I had made up my mind that I didn't want to be the kind of woman who just sits around all day letting life pass me by. What I didn't know was that I was missing much more by *not* letting life pass me by, or at least some of it.

When my daughter came along, I became even more determined to keep my commitment to perfection. I wanted everything done completely and done right. I wanted a perfectly-clean house, perfectly-made meals, perfect children, perfectly-written manuscripts, perfect family time…so I pushed myself even harder.

I did pretty well—until our third child came along. He was a colicky and demanding baby, but he taught me a great deal about what life really is. I can tell you: life is not a perfectly-clean house!

Watching my youngest has made me yearn to bring back the baby days of the other two. I miss their "ooohhhs" and "aaahhs." I miss their early morning giggles when they spotted me from their cribs as I stood in the doorway. I even miss the spilled juice and graham crackers squashed into the hem of my skirt.

Being forced to slow down for my third child has inadvertently forced me to slow down for the other two. It has even forced me to slow down for my husband and myself. I may not have slowed down physically—we still need to eat and wear clean clothes, and there are always deadlines on the horizon—but I've slowed down mentally.

Easing up on the accelerator has allowed me to take a more objective look at our society. What I saw alarmed me. The emphasis is on productivity, activity, and excellence, and we have no time for contemplation. Inactivity and solitude have become dirty words. Spiritual growth, if mentioned at all, is something everybody is always meaning to get around to, but seldom does. Relaxation isn't even relaxing any-more. Rather than nourish the soul, it decays the mind and unsettles the body. So many people are preoccupied with getting somewhere in life that I wonder what will happen when they get there.

I'm not suggesting that we all quit our current lifestyles and become hermits. Work and activity are necessary parts of life. There's nothing wrong with reaching for goals and wanting nice things as long as we know why we want them, what the cost will be to obtain them, and what the consequences will be once we have them. We have to live in the world, but we mustn't allow ourselves to become *of* the world.

During Lent, we're especially called to spiritually center our lives. Lent is a time for reflection, rejuvenation, and revitalization. It's time to put worldly perfection aside and strive more fully for spiritual perfection. Certainly, we can't let all our goals shift; we still have responsibilities in the home and workplace. Yet, we may be able to replace some of our unessential goals with spiritual ones, like setting aside a few minutes each day to meditate upon the passion of our Lord or striving to attend daily Mass. Taking such small strides will lead us to the perfection God meant for us.

I, of course, am not perfect, although I still catch myself trying to be. Then I put the clothes down, push the laundry basket in the corner, and go read the kids a story or pray with them. And *that's* what life is all about.

## What does Scripture say?

*Be perfect, therefore, as your heavenly Father is perfect.*

MATTHEW 5:48

## What does my heart say?

**|** What does the word "perfect" mean to me?
**|** In what areas of my life would I like to be more perfect?
**|** Why is that important to me?

# EASTER

∎ ∎ ∎ ∎ ∎ ∎ ∎ ∎ ∎ ∎ ∎ ∎ ∎ ∎ ∎ ∎ ∎ ∎ ∎ ∎ ∎ ∎ ∎ ∎ ∎ ∎ ∎ ∎ ∎ ∎ ∎ ∎ ∎ ∎

## A Golden Treasure

WE STOOD before his grave, not knowing what to say. On the spur of the moment, I had taken my children to visit my father's grave on the way to see a former high classmate. Matthew, Monica, and Luke, at ages fourteen, eleven, and eight respectively, remembered a little of our last visit. Three-year-old John remembered nothing at all—he had been just an infant when we last came. Now the grave was overgrown with weeds, and the wooden cross with plastic flowers had lost its luster and was leaning precariously to one side.

It was John who got it all started. His many questions led me through the whole scenario of what it was like when I used to live here, of what Grandpa was like, how he died, why his body was buried in this spot, where Grandpa is now...

As I began to tell the stories, Matthew solemnly bent down and began pulling away the weeds. Monica straightened the cross. Luke and John walked around the border of the cemetery looking for treasures to adorn Grandpa's grave; on this open hillside, there was a plethora of artificial bouquets and decorations that had blown away from other graves. I soon found myself plucking along beside them. We worked diligently, reverently, as I unfolded my life with Grandpa for them.

Before long, my father's grave was well-groomed and trimmed

with "new" bouquets. Matthew had fixed the stand for the cross so that it stood erect and gleaming in the sun. We prayed together, and then we stepped back to admire our work.

Soon I found myself driving past the apple orchard my father and I had planned, planted, and cultivated together. How many Saturdays had I spent there with Dad—sometimes in bitter winds, sometimes in sweltering heat—as we shoveled, pruned, mowed, and mulched? He'd tell me stories of his childhood and his time in the Navy and sing me songs from days gone by. There's nothing much left of it now but a gnarled old tree or two. Someone built a house right in the middle of it and let the rest of it go to waste.

We drove past the house I lived in during my high school years. I could again hear my family's voices around the dining room table during our last Christmas together before Dad died. He spent the entire evening telling each of us of his pride and confidence in us, the qualities he saw in us, and of his certainty that we were all capable of making it in life even if he died that very day. He died unexpectedly just three weeks later of congestive heart failure and complications from a stroke. Now the house is a run-down eyesore.

We found ourselves walking on the bridges of the old millpond where I spent hours wandering, writing, and listening to the rush of the water over the falls. It was my place to get away, to be at peace where the world couldn't touch me. Now garbage floats in the water and the mill uses electricity.

Being city kids all their lives, my children were enamored by my life in a small rural community of about two hundred people. They were angry that it had all dissolved before they could experience it themselves.

I was troubled on my way back home that day. My father lived for forty-nine years. In that brief lifespan, he served in the U.S. Navy, attended Marquette University, held a good factory job, married, had four children, built a house with his own hands, bought a second house and a plot of farmland, and moved his family to the country to fulfill his dream of owning an apple orchard. What was left? Some run-down property and a body in a grave.

*Remember that you are dust, and to dust you shall return,* echoed in my mind as I drove along. *Is that all that's become of Dad's life now...dust?*

But I'm left, Dad's memories are left, and my children are left—just as, after Christ's ascension, the apostles were left. I can only imagine the sorrow they must have felt as they said good-bye to their teacher and friend after having spent three years at his side and trembled through his passion. Perhaps they wondered if it had all been worth it when it seemed as though there was nothing left behind, not even some run down property. Not even a body in a grave.

Was there *really* nothing left? There was everything left! The apostles were given the incredible task of nurturing and spreading the newly founded Church. They were assured of the coming of the Holy Spirit. They were guaranteed Christ's presence in the holy Eucharist and the granting of their prayers when two or three gather in his name. They were shown the promise of eternity. Christ would now live in them, through them, and with them.

Dad's not the owner of some dilapidated buildings and an over-grown clump of trees. He's a soul in the presence of God—free of the inhibitions and hardships that plagued him on earth. Because I'm his daughter, he lives in me, through me, and with me as I carry on and share with others all that he's taught me. What's left is the golden treasure of his life that he's passed on to me.

### What does Scripture say?

*So you have pain now; but I will see you again, and your hearts will rejoice, and no one will take your joy from you.*

JOHN 16:22

### What does my heart say?

- **I** What loss in my life has been the most difficult to over-come?
- **I** Have I ever wondered if it was all worth it?
- **I** Do I believe it was worth it now?

▮ ▮ ▮ ▮
# Throwing Stones

PLUNK. "Did you see that, Mama? Did you see it? Lookit!" John squealed as he crouched along the lakeshore. Plunk. My two-and-a-half-yearold threw stone after stone after stone into the water, like a little machine. Plunk. Squeal. Plunk. Squeal. He had created a rhythm, and this was very important business—important enough to wolf down a sticky peanut butter and jelly sandwich in about thirty seconds flat. Without benefit of drink, although he could have had one had he waited long enough. Alas, he had better things to do.

I'd decided we needed a change of scenery, so we packed an impromptu picnic lunch and went to eat down by the water's edge. Eating "down at the lake" is one of the kids' favorite things to do, and it gives John an opportunity to continue his mission: refilling Lake Michigan with every stone that washes ashore.

After about half an hour of plunking, John stood up and handed a stone to me. "You throw it, Mama!"

I smiled, took the stone from his dusty little hand, and tossed it into the water. Plunk. I had to admit it *was* kind of fun. "Did you like that, John?" I asked.

"Yesssss!" he squealed. But when I tried to go back to where I had been sitting, he frowned at me and jabbed another stone at my hand. "Do it again! Do it again!" he demanded.

I smiled and did it again. And again. And again. And again. He wouldn't let me stop. He wanted me to take over his job so that he could rest. Head propped up on his fists, he gleefully settled down to watch Mama work.

As I listened to the plunk-squeal-plunk-squeal rhythm of which I had now become a part, I thought back to the day John was born. We had an emergency cesarean section at just thirty-one weeks gestation, because he had gone limp in utero and wasn't responding to stimulation. I remembered lying in the operating room just after his birth; the room was dreadfully quiet. I knew something was terribly wrong, because my doctor wasn't making light conversation with me the way he had during the births of our other three children—two of whom had also been born prematurely and had been in critical condition. As they were rushed to the neonatal intensive care unit, I had joked with the doctor because it helped to relieve the tension. But this time no one was humoring me by laughing at my stupid jokes. No one would even make eye contact with me.

I asked Mark what was happening.

"Just wait," he said as he squeezed tighter on my already icy hand. I knew now that our new little son was in grave danger.

I laid back, closed my eyes, and silently hissed at God, "You really ARE going to do this, aren't you? You're going to do this to me a THIRD time! How could you?" I waited for what seemed an eternity longer, but still no one spoke.

Unable to bear the silence a second more, I called out across the room to the neonatologist who was working feverishly over John. "Doctor, how is he?"

The doctor abruptly straightened up, paused, took a deep breath, and then answered, "Well, he's having a bit of trouble just now, but we're doing everything we can."

I laid back and again hissed at God, "You're going to take him, aren't you?"

It was a long recovery for John. He spent a month hooked up to IV needles, respirators, catheters, feeding tubes, scopes, and monitors. He went into crisis a few times, but his guardian angel and watchful nurses kept him from demise. He was quite sickly the first two years of his life, returning to the hospital once and spending countless nights in the emergency room, but he made it. And now I can take him down to the shore to throw stones until his heart's content.

I often wonder about John's peculiar beginning. What was God's point? I mean, didn't I learn whatever lesson he wanted to teach me the first time? Second time? Have I learned it the third time? I had already said "yes" to the heavenly Father when our first child was given a slim chance of survival after birth. I said "yes" when our second child brushed with death and nearly lost the fight. Why was it necessary to say "yes" again?

I don't know the answer. But I do know that somehow, I'm a bit stronger because of it. It's helped me to truly appreciate the sorrow of others. I don't just sympathize; I empathize. When friends call me with desperate stories, I can listen with an understanding heart and offer them support and a promise of prayer. I know well the prayer of a distraught child of the Father because I've prayed it many times myself.

Apparently, it was necessary for me to say "yes" again. I had to experience the turmoil and sorrow just as the disciples did during Christ's passion. I've had to keep walking along the road to Emmaus, rehashing all that's happened until my Lord comes along and reveals his truth to me. I know the heavenly Father has a plan for me—for each one of us—and that it is a good plan, whether or not it answers to human reason. Perhaps the reason is more complicated than I'm able to comprehend. Perhaps the reason is too simple for me to see. Or perhaps God kept that flicker of life going, just so John could throw stones along the shore.

## What does Scripture say?

*Now on that same day two of them were going to a village called Emmaus, about seven miles from Jerusalem, and talking with each other about all these things that had happened. While they were talking and discussing, Jesus himself came near and went with them…*

LUKE 24:13–15

## What does my heart say?

I When have I felt like the disciples on the way to Emmaus?

I When have I suffered a loss that was later restored?

I What is my response when God asks me to say yes repeatedly to something I'm not willing to accept?

∎ ı ı ∎
# Whymania

LUKE'S BEEN SMITTEN by a childhood illness with no known cure. It's a debilitating sickness that hits when you least expect it. My once normal three-year-old has contracted Whymania, an evil disease that impairs the victim's mental abilities, allowing accessibility to a single cognitive word: why.

Gone are the days when Luke would busy himself with coloring books and pretend dragons. Gone are the days when he would sit still in the back seat of the car singing quietly to himself. Gone are the days when we could complete a simple trip to the market for milk in less than four hours. Gone. All gone.

Now he spends all of his waking hours in a foggy haze, mumbling the word "why" at everything he sees and hears. The worst part of this chronic condition is that Whymania affects everyone with whom Luke comes into contact, turning them into blubbering fools or zombies who stare off into space.

It's a shame what it did to the student nurse during Luke's last checkup.

"Why me up here?" he asked as he peered over the edge of the examination table.

"Why you listen to my heart?" Luke asked as he leaned forward, squinting into the startled man's face.

"Why you shake so much?" Luke prodded, pointing to his unsteady hands.

"Why you use dat ting?" he insisted as the nurse fumbled with the stethoscope.

"Ah. Um. Wha," replied the nurse as his trembling became uncontrollable and a daze slipped across his face.

There's a woman somewhere out there who's probably convinced that I'm ready for the insane asylum. Two weeks ago at the library, Luke's disease became quite bad.

"Why dis book green, Mom? Why all dese books here, Mom?

Why we come here, Mom?" Luke quizzed me.

I was in a terrible hurry that day and not in the mood to cope with this affliction. "Oh, Luke!" I blurted out. "Please stop! I don't have any more answers! Mom's answers are all used up!"

I heard a sudden shuffle on the other side of the aisle and saw a set of eyes peering at me from behind *Jane Brody's Nutrition Book, Updated.* The eyes made their way down the shelf until a shocked-looking middle-aged woman scurried around the corner, shaking her head.

But the clincher came one morning not long ago when we ventured out after a spring rain. Whymania had a griping hold on Luke that morning. "Why it rained, Mom?" he asked.

"Because God wanted to water the flowers."

"Why it stopped raining, Mom?"

"Because God decided the flowers had enough water."

"Why the flowers in our garden?"

"Because God made them."

"Why God made the flowers?"

"Because he loves us."

I stopped in my tracks, suddenly hit by my own words. It had never occurred to me before that God would show his love through something as simple as a flower. Eons ago, God had known that Luke and I would be standing there at that very moment battling a harsh bout with Whymania and contemplating the existence of a group of lovely tulips. In his omnipotent wisdom, he allowed them to grow there as a reminder of his love for us—beautiful crimson tulips, placed there so that Luke and I could behold them and Luke could "why" about them.

Perhaps Easter is a good time for us to contract our own case of Whymania. How many times have we heard the story of the resurrection? How many times have we run to the tomb with Peter, only to find it empty? How many times have we felt the sadness of the women as they sought the risen Christ's body? How many times did we hear the voices of the apostles as they wondered how such a miracle could have taken place? Yet, I would imagine that during those times, we have seldom if ever asked, "Why?"

The answer has a lot to do with the crimson tulips Luke and I encountered on a rainy spring day. They're symbolic of the long, cold winter and the glorious rising to new life. They're a reminder of God's miraculous power to renew and of his eternal love for us. Like Luke's curiosity about the tulips, the resurrection causes us to ask, "Why?"

Because he loves us.

## What does Scripture say?

*[T]he LORD appeared to him from far away. I have loved you with an everlasting love; therefore I have continued my faithfulness to you.*

JEREMIAH 31:3

## What does my heart say?

I When was the last time I discovered a "crimson tulip" in my life?

I Why did the heavenly Father send it at that place and time?

I What are the symbols of his resurrection around me?

∎ ∎ ∎ ∎

# Everybody, Duck!

WORKING THINGS OUT before the Blessed Sacrament makes me feel as though I'm sitting in private consultation with our Lord. When I pray before his real presence displayed in the monstrance, I forget about everything around me. Then it's just the two of us—head to head, discussing, weighing, evaluating, and contemplating. Even though our Lord always listens to my prayers no matter where I pray or at what time of day I say them, spending time with him in eucharistic adoration is vastly different.

There was a situation weighing particularly heavy on my heart for which ducks had become symbolic to me. Earlier that summer, I had been sitting at the lakeshore while on vacation when a flock of duck families landed right in front of me. The way the duck families complimented one another helped me to see the way people needed to work together in the situation that was bothering me.

On this day when things seemed especially bothersome, I went to my favorite place to pray—the Schoenstatt Marian Shrine near my home—so I could spend time "discussing" things with our Lord present in the Eucharist. Consequently, I was spending considerable time and energy tossing around thoughts of webbed feet, feathered wings, and wide, yellow bills. As I was praying and mashing things out, a friend of mine came in and genuflected. Moving past me to her pew, she handed me a CD with a little card attached that bore a picture of a pond. I looked closer and smiled. There was a duck swimming in the middle of the pond. Amazing! It seemed that our Lord was giving me direct confirmation for my petition. I jubilantly thanked him, finished my Holy Hour, and prepared to leave.

Before I left, I whispered a thank you in my friend's ear and told her that she had delivered a symbolic message from Jesus for me. Curious, she followed me out of the shrine. Outside, I explained that ducks were a symbol for me in regard to a troubling situation about which I was praying.

"But that's not a duck," she said.

"What is it, then?" I asked disappointedly.

"I don't know," she replied. "I think it's a frog."

I sighed and knitted my brow, hoping that squinting might transform the frog into a duck. It didn't work.

"Oh, well. At least it reminded me of a duck," I said in self-consolation.

We headed for the parking lot and walked to our cars. I got in and reached over to start the engine. I jumped when I heard a knock on my window. There stood my friend, with a glowing smile on her face.

"There are your ducks!" she said excitedly, pointing to a spot about twenty feet in front of my van.

There in the backyard adjacent to the parking lot was a live mother duck with six tiny ducklings waddling along behind her. Not only were the two of us in awe of this unusual sight, but the members of that household and some of the neighbors on either side of the property had gathered to take in the spectacle also.

If I hadn't had a witness, I probably wouldn't have believed it myself. I stood awestruck, watching them. Mother duck was totally oblivious to our presence as she waddled around routinely tending to her ducklings. Little did she know that it was abnormal to see a family of ducks in the back yard of a mid-city neighborhood. The inexplicable arrival of the ducks in that backyard reminded me of the day I'd been watching the families of ducks at the lake. The way they'd worked together and solved their problems together was the way the problem agitating my heart would have to be solved.

This little miracle was a "resurrection moment" for me. A resurrection moment is that "zing" in your heart when you're suddenly pulled out of your closed, human way of thinking and uplifted into another realm. It's our Lord's way of reminding us that no situation large or small is beyond his power to transform and renew. He can convince a mother duck and her six ducklings to land in a mid-city neighborhood; he can make his torn and tattered body rise from the dead.

Of course, Easter is the greatest resurrection moment of all. After spending an entire Lent tossing around thoughts of webbed feet, winged feathers and wide, yellow bills, we awaken on Easter morning to find the whole duck family waddling around in our own backyard.

## What does Scripture say?

*And the one who was seated on the throne said, "See, I am making all things new." Also he said, "Write this, for these words are trustworthy and true." Then he said to me, "It is done! I am the Alpha and the Omega, the beginning and the end. To the thirsty I will give water as a gift from the spring of the water of life."*

REVELATION 21:5–6

## What does my heart say?

▌ What are one or two of the resurrection moments in my life?
▌ How did our Lord make all things new to me in those situations?
▌ What comes to my mind as I contemplate the risen Christ as the Alpha and the Omega?

∎ ∎ ∎
# Sing "Mary Nodded"

"SING 'MARY NODDED,'" Luke pleaded as I tucked the kids into bed. Although my crooning abilities leave much to be desired, the kids still try to squeeze a song out of me before bed. Either they have tin ears, or they've caught on to the fact that mom's mediocre singing allows them to stay up a few minutes later. It's probably a little of both.

"Um, 'Mary Nodded'?" I asked. "Do you mean 'The Little Drummer Boy'?"

"No! No! 'Mary Nodded'!" Luke was obviously perturbed by my inability to understand his three-year-old dialect. I implored the help of Monica, our family translator.

"He means the one about the lady in the cape, Mom," she said in all of her five-year-old wisdom.

"Cape?" My brain searched my limited repertoire of bedtime songs.

"Mom, you know, the one about the Blessed Mother on the boat!" Matthew almost shouted at me. At eight, he still expected his mom to know everything.

Hmmmmm. Mary wearing a cape on a boat, nodding. "Oh! You mean 'Protect Us With Your Mantle,'" I said, hopefully.

"Yeah!" they chorused. I was delighted to find that my parenthood-plagued mind was still intact.

I smiled to myself as I imagined what might be pictured in my children's minds—our dear Blessed Mother, draped in a Little Red Riding Hood-type cape, sitting in the middle of a dented-up rowboat and nodding in time to something along the lines of "Won't You Be My Neighbor?" or "Three Blind Mice."

I was most interested in the way the kids had recalled the song. They hadn't been concerned with the words—it was the images the song had conjured up (certainly not my singing).

I started thinking about all the titles we Catholics have given to the Blessed Mother. They're mere words, but they conjure up powerful images. Members of The Apostolic Movement of Schoenstatt call her Mother Thrice Admirable, Queen and Victress. Others call her Queen of Peace, Mother of Perpetual Help, Seat of Wisdom, Mother of Sorrows, Star of the Sea, Key of Heaven, and Mystical Rose, for example.

One image that particularly intrigues me is found in the Book of Genesis. It's not absolutely evident that this scene refers to the Blessed Virgin Mary, but some scholars think a direct comparison can be made: "I will put enmity between you and the woman, and between your offspring and hers; he will strike your head, and you will strike his heel" (Genesis 3:15).

In this passage, it's clear that the opposition is not only between Satan and Christ, but also between Satan and the Blessed Virgin Mary. Redemption won't occur without her cooperation. Popes of the past have written about this.

In *Jucunda Semper,* in 1894, Pope Leo XIII described Mary's selfless adherence to God's will: "When Mary offered herself completely to God together with her Son in the temple, she was already sharing with him the painful atonement on behalf of the human race. It is certain, therefore, that she suffered in the very depths of her soul with his most bitter sufferings and with his torments. Finally, it was before the eyes of Mary the Divine Sacrifice for which she had born and nurtured the victim, was to be finished…we see that there stood by the cross of Jesus his mother, who in a miracle of charity, so that she might receive us as her sons, willingly offered him up to divine justice, dying with him in her heart, pierced with the sword of sorrow."

Pope Benedict XV explains it this way in *Inter Sodalicia*: "To such an extent did [Mary] suffer and almost die with her suffering and dying Son; to such extent did she surrender her maternal rights over her Son for man's salvation, and immolated Him—insofar as she could—in order to appease the justice of God, that we rightly say she redeemed the human race together with Christ" (Apostolic Letter *Inter Sodalicia*; *AAS* 10 [1918]).

Pope John Paul II states in *Salvifici Doloris*: "In her, the many and intense sufferings were amassed in such an interconnected way that they were not only a proof of her unshakable faith, but also a contribution to the redemption of all.....It was on Calvary that Mary's suffering, beside the suffering of Jesus, reached an intensity that can hardly be imagined from a human point of view, but which was mysteriously and supernaturally fruitful for the redemption of the world. Her ascent of Calvary and her standing at the foot of the cross together with the beloved disciple were a special sort of sharing in the redeeming death of her son."

Imagine, she surrendered her maternal rights so that we might achieve eternal salvation. She didn't even know us then! And yet she remained silent while her son was whipped, mocked, spit upon, and nailed to the cross.

I'm not certain whether it's the Blessed Mother's incredible self-surrender to the will of God or her unfathomable love for humankind that strikes me most. Like my children, I have an image of her indelibly etched into my mind—that of the woman who joins with her offspring to oppose Satan. Without her "yes," there would be no Good Friday and in turn no Easter Sunday.

## What does Scripture say?

*"I will put enmity between you and the woman,*
*and between your offspring and hers;*
*he will strike your head,*
*and you will strike his heel."*

GENESIS 3:15

## What does my heart say?

- **|** What comes to my mind when I think about the Blessed Virgin Mary?
- **|** Is there a specific image of her that comes to mind?
- **|** Can I imagine the way she experienced the joy of the resurrection?

■ I I ■

# Easter Joy

HE SAT, his round little cheeks slung into his plump little hands and his elbows propped sullenly up on the dining room table. Our poor little John-John was a truly unhappy camper. "You guys think that, just because I'm five years old, that I can't go to confession. But I have sins, too, and I want to go to confession!" he blurted out desperately.

Oh, my. His outburst caught us all by surprise. Our family had been discussing going to confession on the coming Saturday, never realizing that John had any interest in the conversation at all. Granted, he'd been asking us to go to confession on and off over the past year, but we thought that it had more to do with his infatuation with the confessional than any lean toward piety. Whenever the family went to confession, he always asked to go along. Once there, he'd ask to be able to get in line also. We'd calmly explain that he was too young to go and would have to wait until he was older. He'd heave a sigh and slide back into the pew, knowing he was facing a long, boring wait.

It was obvious this time that John wasn't going to let us get away with depriving him of the sacrament of reconciliation. He stood his ground and looked me right in the eye.

"Well, John," I tried to coax. "It isn't as easy as all that. If you really want to go to confession, you'll have to learn a few things first."

"Like what?" he asked suspiciously.

"Like what to do and what to say. You'll need to know the 'Act of Contrition' and what absolution means. You'll need to learn how to make a good examination of conscience. And, you'll need to understand what a penance is and what it means when the priest acts *in persona Christi*," I said, referring to the Catholic belief of the priest as representative of Jesus Christ and trying to make it sound as complicated as possible.

"Okay," he said, blinking his hazel eyes attentively. "Can you teach me right now?"

Although he was younger than the usual age for receiving the sacrament, his desire was so strong that we decided we'd better act on it. We petitioned our parish priest, explaining to him that we believed John's intent to be genuine and assuring him that John would be prepared prudently and responsibly. At the end of the consult, he gave us special permission to begin preparation.

John was a dedicated student. He learned all he needed to know and within a few weeks, he received the sacrament of reconciliation for the first time. How proud he was as he walked back to us afterward, holding the priest's hand! His face was one huge smile and his eyes sparkled with elation. Finally, he was able to do what he had so longed to do—pour out his overflowing heart to his Savior and experience the joy of forgiveness.

Children instinctively know what is righteous and holy and are compelled toward forgiveness. Have you ever seen a child trying to hide something he's done wrong? Somehow it always works its way out, no matter how hard the child tries to keep it in. They know that once the hard part is over—once they've admitted their guilt—they'll be able to make amends and enjoy the peace of a cleared conscience.

During these past weeks of Lent, the Church compelled us to seek forgiveness and take the opportunity to pour out our overflowing hearts to our Savior. We reflected upon our weaknesses and failures. We fasted, sacrificed, and gave alms. We repented and attempted to atone for our sins. We walked the way of the cross with our Lord, contemplated his agony, and were reminded that it was our sins for which he suffered and died. The Church reminded us during this penitential season that we are children of God and encouraged us to make amends so that we can enjoy the peace of a cleared conscience. The hard part is over. Even if, in our humanness, we were irresolute in our repentance, we are still forgiven. Why? It's because Jesus carried the cross in our place. His passion has been completed, and he is risen.

Now it's time to follow John's example by going forward with huge smiles on our faces and elation in our hearts. Now it's time for Easter joy.

## What does Scripture say?

*Arise, shine; for your light has come, and the glory of the LORD has risen upon you. For darkness shall cover the earth, and thick darkness the peoples; but the LORD will arise upon you, and his glory will appear over you.*

ISAIAH 60:1–2

## What does my heart say?

▍ What was my way of the cross like this Lent?
▍ How have I prepared to experience Easter joy?
▍ How can I share that Easter joy with others?

∎ ı ı ∎

# They'll Know We Are Christians

I'LL NEVER FORGET the song, "They'll Know We Are Christians By Our Love." I sang it countless times as a young girl attending St. Philip Neri Catholic Grade School in Milwaukee. Our pastor, Father Aloysius Ahler, insisted on every student knowing the songs that we were expected to sing at daily holy Mass, and that song was one of them.

Father Ahler was a stickler for piety and form and used his baritone voice frequently to "whip" us into shape. If we weren't singing with the proper pitch and enthusiasm, Father would yell to the organist to stop. "I can't hear you!" he'd bellow from behind the altar as we instantly sunk as low as we could in the pews. Once he'd sufficiently gotten his point across, he'd resume. "All right, let's try it again." He'd rumble down the aisle, and the organ would wail as we did our best to convince the people passing by on the street that they would *know* we were Christians by our love.

Some people—parents and students alike—didn't care for Father Ahler's fire-and-brimstone approach. I thrived on it. He was tough and intimidating at times, but not out of cruelty. He pushed us hard because of his profound appreciation of our holy faith. When he said holy Mass, you paid attention because he commanded respect—not for himself, but for our Savior in the holy Eucharist. Woe to the boy or girl who was caught fidgeting at the Communion rail. That happened to my friend's eighth grade brother once. The kid was so shaken when Father Ahler caught and chastised him for goofing off that he fainted. None of us was even tempted to goof off at the Communion rail after that. Forgetting to bless oneself upon entering the church or forgetting to genuflect before entering the pew would bring a howling reprimand. Father wanted us to be constantly aware of the tremendous undertaking we had begun by calling ourselves Catholic, and I loved him for it.

In spite of his bulldog exterior, Father Ahler had an interior kindness that could be sensed, even while he was scolding a child. Never did he fail to make us understand that his anger was not for us, but for the action. He was quick with a warm smile as he made his way over the playground during recess. Pipe crooked carefully at the side of his mouth, biretta perched atop his head, and hands clasped precisely behind his black cassock, he paced steadily through the chaos like a gentleman farmer admiring his crops.

I'm happy to say that I'm a product of those crops. Father Ahler imparted to me a profound devotion to the holy Eucharist. He also was instrumental in deepening the love for the Blessed Mother that began in me when Father Kentenich, founder of The Apostolic Movement of Schoenstatt, dedicated me to her as an infant. In founding the parish, Father Ahler invited the Schoenstatt Sisters of Mary to teach at the school. He built a convent for them and a Schoenstatt Marian Shrine on the playground. I became acquainted with the Blessed Mother there, soaking in her loveliness during nearly every recess. Had I not had access to the shrine, I doubt my love for her would have grown so deeply at such a young age.

Someone discovered that love in me recently through a message I had posted on an email list. I wrote the message for a couple who had a critically-ill newborn. Having been through that same scenario three times myself, I had some thoughts and encouragement that I wanted to pass on to them.

I explained that, in my helplessness of waiting for my child to either live or die, I cried out to the Blessed Mother for strength and consolation. I played a mental game with myself, imagining her standing before me as I pleaded the needs of my little one. I would put her in charge, asking her (as only she in her miraculous way can do) to reach through the walls of the isolette to hold and soothe my child because I could not. Then I would picture the Blessed Mother scooping up and comforting my baby. That was the only peace I could attain during those awful months. And I had learned to reach for that peace in the quiet moments I spent in the shrine at St. Philip Neri Catholic Grade School.

A few days after I sent that email message, I received one from another mom in Texas. She had seen the message, noticed my name, and wondered if I was involved in the Schoenstatt Movement. Imagine my astonishment. How had she known? I had never mentioned the word Schoenstatt in my message. This mom said she could tell I belonged to the Marian movement by my love for the Blessed Mother. She, too, was a member of the movement.

She knew me by my love.

It's not necessary to belong to the Schoenstatt Movement in order to have that kind of love for the Blessed Mother—it's the calling of all Christians. Christ and his mother are inseparable; we can't love one without loving the other. As modern day apostles, we must daringly demonstrate that love. We courageously live out the Acts of the Apostles so that all will *know* that we are Christians by our love.

## What does Scripture say?

*See what love the Father has given us, that we should be called children of God; and that is what we are. The reason the world does not know us is that it did not know him. We know love by this, that he laid down his life for us—and we ought to lay down our lives for one another.*

1 JOHN 3:1, 16

## What does my heart say?

❙ What does the word "Christian" mean to me?
❙ What kind of love do Christians show?
❙ How will others know me by my love?

■ ▮ ▮ ■

# God's Herb Garden

I HAVE AN INDOOR HERB GARDEN in my kitchen window. That's quite surprising, considering I'm on the UBP's Most Wanted list. UBP stands for Universal Botanical Police, and they want me because I'm a known plant killer. However, in spite of my criminal ways, these agricultural midgets manage to survive. Like my children, they continue to grow without the slightest provocation.

I love my fragrant little wonders. They were so easy to grow! I grabbed a couple of pots from my basement collection leftover from deceased philodendrons, roughed up the soil, sprinkled a few seeds, scratched at the dirt a bit with my fingers, poured in some water, and begged God's mercy on them. Within a week or so, tiny green heads began to wind their way up out of the soil. A couple of more weeks, and they sprouted luscious, tangy leaves. I thinned out the plants and I water them whenever I wash down the kitchen counters. If I remember, that is. If I even wash down the kitchen counters. I'm sure now you understand why the UBP wants me.

The way my herbs grow is remarkable. My small kitchen window allows them a limited view of the sun. They make the most of the available sunlight by reaching toward the window. Because I'm a symmetry fanatic, I can't stand to have herbs that lean to one side. So, I trick them. When they've leaned their farthest, assuring themselves a huge gulping of sunlight, I turn the pots around so they're facing the opposite direction. Alas, the poor little things. In their insistence on finding the sun, they begin their struggle all over again. Within a few days, they're reaching once again toward the window, begging the sun to warm them up. Then I deviously turn the pots again, and again they reach. Turn. Reach. Turn. Reach.

As their leaves flourish, I strategically pick the largest ones, heartlessly crushing them between my fingers and tossing them into a pot of simmering spaghetti sauce or scattering them over a fresh salad. No matter how I pluck, new leaves appear over and over and over again.

Perhaps I enjoy my little herb plants so much because they remind me of myself. I was once nothing more than a tiny seed God planted in his herb garden. When he poured forth his grace, I grew a stem, branches, and leaves. He carefully placed me in front of his kitchen window—the Blessed Virgin Mary—so I could prosper and serve him. Like my agricultural midgets, I incessantly reach toward that window in order to soak up the valuable Son light.

In general, I like being one of God's little herb plants. I like the feeling of stretching out my stem so I can feel the warmth of the Son coming through the window. I thrive when he takes his watering can and pours his grace all over me. It's so cool and refreshing.

I loathe it when my pot gets turned around. When I'm suddenly facing the darkness of ungodly thinking, despair and sin, I feel afraid and confused. Then I have to again begin my struggle to reach toward the Son. Sometimes lack of time and understanding turns around my pot. Sometimes my own spiritual laziness and negligence turn my pot around. No matter what the cause, my pot gets turned around more often than I'd like to admit. It takes concentrated effort to crank my stem around and begin growing back toward the window.

I'm not too enthused about having my leaves torn off and crushed, either. When God makes spaghetti, the end results are always fabulous, but giving up a part of myself as an ingredient is downright painful. He's done a lot of Italian cooking in our house this past year, and especially during this past Lent. Each time he wanted a larger leaf than the time before. I lost a multitude when our youngest child, John, was born prematurely and nearly died. I lost an entire branch during his hospitalization. I lost several limbs, shaking my stem right down to my roots, as John was later re-hospitalized with pneumonia. I felt myself begin to whither when the doctor told me that John had a potentially life threatening condition that required major surgery. The Master Gardener rushed to my rescue with his watering can as the doctors reexamined John and decided that the condition would not require surgery after all. There were many other pots of spaghetti— hurtful relationships, physical hardships, and the wear and tear of parenting.

But like my little herb plants, I winced at the initial pain only to later experience new growth. God was generous with his watering can and showered me with his graces, fulfilling in me the fruits of the resurrection. By watching my own indoor herbs, I've come to realize that I'm only of any real use to the Master Gardener if I allow him to tear off my leaves, crush them, and toss them into the simmering pot of spaghetti. I've learned that he'll be there with his watering can before I whither, and he'll never pluck more leaves and branches than I can bear to lose. It may be painful, but the results will be fabulous.

## What does Scripture say?

> *They shall come and sing aloud on the height of Zion, and they shall be radiant over the goodness of the* LORD, *over the grain, the wine, and the oil, and over the young of the flock and the herd; their life shall become like a watered garden, and they shall never languish again.*
>
> JEREMIAH 31:12

## What does my heart say?

**I** When have I needed to turn from darkness into light?

**I** What is my initial response when the Master Gardener tears off my biggest leaves?

**I** How would I like to respond the next time he makes spaghetti?

# ORDINARY TIME

■ I I I ■ I I I I ■ I I I I I ■ I I I I I ■ I I I I I ■ I I I I I ■

## When's God Gonna Show Up?

WE'RE FORTUNATE to belong to a parish that has eucharistic adoration every Thursday from 8:00 AM to 8:00 PM. On a recent Thursday, the Director of Religious Education invited all of the students of the third grade through high school level and their parents to attend the last hour of adoration as part of a closing ceremony for the school year. Our third grader, Matthew, was encouraged to attend with his class. However, Mark and I thought it would be a great opportunity for our whole family to learn more about the Eucharist, and so we brought along our first grader, Monica, and our preschooler, Luke.

In our best effort to simplify one of the greatest mysteries of our Catholic faith, we explained to our six-year-old and four-year-old that our Lord would be present there for us in a special way. He would be waiting there to listen to anything we would have to tell him, any worries we would like to share with him, any petitions we would like to lay before him. He would be there in his entire being: body, blood, soul, and divinity.

The church looked exceptionally beautiful as we entered. All the candles were lit on both of the altars, giving the building a special glow in the fading daylight. The monstrance stood on the high altar, glistening before the dozens of little flames that surrounded it. With Monica kneeling next to me and Luke perched on Mark's lap, we settled into our pew, prepared for a religious experience that would have a profound effect on our little children's minds and hearts. I was exuberant as I watched Monica and Luke's eyes dance in the beauty of the candlelight, and I supposed that their pure little souls were being lifted to the heights of spiritual ecstasy. We knelt there in silence for a moment, gazing at the monstrance and taking in the glorious atmosphere.

As we waited for the deacon to begin leading the rosary, Luke began tugging mercilessly on Mark's neck.

"Dad! Dad!" he whisper-shouted excitedly.

"Sssh." Mark warned.

"Dad! Dad-dy!" Luke persisted.

"What is it?" Mark asked him.

Losing all of his whisper to unrestrained frustration, Luke shot out, "When's God gonna show up?"

I'm not certain what Mark replied to Luke, because I was too busy pulling my sunken heart back up into my chest cavity. How could we have fouled up so badly in preparing our children for this miraculous moment? Luke appeared to be completely clueless about what was going on. I watched as his eyes grew increasingly rounder while Mark whispered an explanation into his ear. I imagined he was trying to figure out how the priest had taken an entire human being and stuffed it into a glass capsule three inches in diameter.

"Hopeless," I said to myself. "He'll never get it." And then I wondered how much I myself had absorbed over the years. While not in the same circumstance, there have been many times in my life that I've wondered, "When's God gonna show up?"

The day eighteen years ago when the doctor came rushing into the hospital waiting room and clumsily blurted out that my father was dead, I wondered, "When's God gonna show up?" As I laid in the preoperative room at the hospital nine years ago listening to a neonatologist tell me that the baby I was about to give birth to had just a fifty-percent chance of survival, I wondered, "When's God gonna show up?" Two years later, the maternal-fetal specialist informed me that the tiny person inside my womb would soon miscarry, and I wondered, "When's God gonna show up?" A bit more than a year after that, I sat in the neonatal intensive care unit as my baby girl barely clung to life and bitterly sputtered, "When's God gonna show up?" Last summer I stood in the middle of our new "dream home" looking at the filth and destruction the previous owners had caused out of vengeance for us, wondering, "When's God gonna show up?"

I've even wondered about him during the day-to-day trials. When the kids are screaming, the supper is scorched, I've got a deadline to meet, and the dog's gagging something up in the corner, I cry out, "When's God gonna show up?" Someone very close to me has done something that's hurt me deeply and I whine, "When's God gonna show up?" Matthew needs help with his homework, Monica's got gum in her hair, Luke's coming down with something, we need to be somewhere in an hour, and I demand, "When's God gonna show up?"

If I, as a mature Catholic, wonder about God's presence in my life, why should I be surprised that Luke can't immediately see him in the monstrance? I should know better, but still I sometimes doubt. It seems that, through the years, I wasn't waiting for God to show up; he was waiting for me to show up.

## What does Scripture say?

> *Create in me a clean heart, O God,*
> *and put a new and right spirit within me.*
> *Do not cast me away from your presence,*
> *and do not take your holy spirit from me.*
> *Restore to me the joy of your salvation,*
> *and sustain in me a willing spirit.*
>
> PSALM 51:10–12

## What does my heart say?

**I** When in my life have I wondered, "When's God gonna show up?"

**I** How did he show up?

**I** How can I maintain a "clean heart" even in times of uncertainty?

▮ ▮ ▮ ▮
# A Real Intellectual

SOME YEARS AGO, my mother-in-law gave Mark and me a box of books that had belonged to my father-in-law. We were so happy to have something of his possessions. There wasn't much left from Dad, and a little had to go a long way among a family of twelve children. Being a teacher, books were important to him. So having something this special from Dad not only gave us a remembrance of him, but a connection to who he was as an individual.

I remember pandering through the titles, wondering what Dad might have thought as he read them. Because Dad died before Mark and I were introduced, I've longed to become acquainted with the father-in-law I never met.

I stopped at one book in particular, *Mary in the New Testament,* and flipped through the pages. "Hmm…pretty heady stuff," I chuckled to myself. "What was he doing with a book like this? A real intellectual, eh?"

Over time, Dad's books have wound their way around various bookshelves, nooks, and crannies. I can't say that I've read them all in earnest, but it's comforting to know that they're here—a symbol of our ongoing relationship with Dad.

This fall, I entered the Certificate in Marian Studies program at the International Marian Research Institute. Studying at a pontifical institute was beyond my wildest dreams, and I found this gift from God to be nothing short of miraculous. I was nervous about how this would unfold; nonetheless I forged ahead. When my instructor gave me the list of books I needed to get started, one of the titles sounded vaguely familiar.

"Maybe we have that one," I thought. "I wonder…" I pooh-poohed the idea and continued my search to find copies of the books I could borrow in order to save money. With the opportunity at the institute having come up so suddenly, I had no budget whatsoever from which to work. I actually found not one, but two copies of the main resource book to borrow. Praise God! Still, that other title kept haunting me.

One morning, I couldn't stand it any longer; I had to find out for sure if that was one of the books from Dad. I grabbed a chair, climbed up, and started pilfering through the bookshelf. I went through pile after pile and then…there it was. In the back of the topmost shelf was a well-worn volume with a red cover. The title was *Mary in the New Testament.*

"A real intellectual, eh?" I chided myself. "Ha. This is Dad's joke on me for being so audacious."

Then the tears came. It was as if this wonderful father was reaching out from heaven and doing what every wonderful father wants to do for his children—helping me along with my education. Suddenly I felt his love in a very tangible way.

I eased myself onto the chair and sat there for a few minutes, holding the book on my lap. I wanted to thank Dad, but didn't know how. All I had to offer was a meager, "Gee. Thanks, Dad." That seemed so inadequate compared to the favor he had just granted me. On the other hand, what more *could* I offer him?

That's how it is with the heavenly Father, also. As any wonderful father, he wants to help his children with their education. Sometimes the learning transpires in the midst of turmoil and confusion, and sometimes it's enveloped in jubilation and excitement. Sometimes it's little more than a subtle, personal revelation that whispers to us out of the blue, like a well-worn red volume on the back of the bookshelf.

## What does Scripture say?

*Who is like the wise man?*
*And who knows the interpretation of a thing?*
*Wisdom makes one's face shine,*
*and the hardness of one's countenance is changed.*

ECCLESIASTES 8:1

## What does my heart say?

- ▌ What is the difference between education and understanding?
- ▌ Which of those do I value more highly? Why?
- ▌ At what levels of education and understanding am I at in my life right now?

▌ ▌ ▌ ▌

# Did You Substitute?

"DID YOU SUBSTITUTE?" That's the first thing the kids ask me when they're about to eat something I've made. They poke around in it a bit, suspiciously eye the counters and cupboards looking for evidence, and then take a circumspect nibble. Their suspicion is reasonable; I tend to be as experimental in the kitchen as I am at the keyboard. There isn't a recipe on earth that I can't find some way to rewrite and edit.

My substitution habit started when the kids were quite small. Being the conscientious mother that I am, I wanted my family to eat healthy. I looked for every possible opportunity to replace less healthy ingredients with more healthy ones. Gradually, I figured out how to make everything with whole foods and without sugars or refined products. My American ingenuity convinced me that if I can make it healthier, I can make it cheaper and faster, too. Thus, the unrelenting cycle began.

The whole-wheat flour wasn't so bad. Sure, baked goods were a bit heavier, a little drier, but they were *healthy* by golly. Then there was the tofu. I tried to slice, bread, and fry it, but it lost its consistency and ended up more like jellied soybean oatmeal. But, hey, it was low fat, wasn't it? Oh, then there was the TVP, or texturized vegetable protein. TVP is a remarkable foodstuff that comes in either chunks or small granules with a high protein value. When it absorbs liquid, it triples its volume and is supposed to take on the flavor of the other ingredients. To this day, Matt scours every soup, casserole, and stir-fry for evidence of TVP. He swears he can detect that stuff a mile away and refuses to have anything to do with it. The best by far are my bean-burgers. They were supposed to be a low-cost vegetarian replacement for ground beef burgers. Instead, they turned out to be crumbly, disgusting blobs of… you don't want to know. Even *I* didn't like them. But they sure were good for you, even if they didn't taste good.

Eventually, I backed off of the whole foods and reintroduced sugars and refined products into our diets. I hadn't given up my determination to feed my family healthy foods; I just wanted them to actually eat the foods I made. On the other hand, my infatuation with substitution seemed to continually increase over the years. It was fun to play around with recipes. I loved trying to find out what would happen if I changed this or that. Missing an ingredient or two (or three) didn't stop me from making something I'd chosen. Sometimes I felt I didn't have the time to do every step listed in the cookbook, and so I took shortcuts. I could give in on the health foods point, but my creativity had to go unleashed.

Most of my concoctions are actually better than the original recipes. Well, that's what *I* think, anyway. I managed to come up with some fantastic new dishes that my family really liked. The problem is, I never write anything down, so I can't repeat the recipes that turn out fantastic. Ergo, my cooking turns out best when I stick to conventional foods and follow prescribed recipes.

My kids are justified in quizzing me before they taste my cooking. They've been "had" too many times in the past—TVP lurking behind the penne rigate, mutilated soybeans nestled under the ketchup, tofu squishing out from behind the broccoli, cake that looks delicious but has the consistency of sawdust imbedded in plaster. The dish may look wonderful, but the taste and texture are undesirable. Or, it may look threatening but taste exquisite. You never know what creations my substitutions will generate.

My penchant for substituting makes me think about the sacraments of the Catholic Church. There is no substitution.

Consider how the Eucharist nourishes and sustains us. Without it we couldn't survive spiritually, and the more often we receive it, the stronger our souls become. There are substitutes—we can make a spiritual Communion or attend a Holy Hour of adoration, but there's nothing like the real thing. What about reconciliation? We could try to get by with saying, "I'm sorry" to our Lord on our own, but unless we receive the full sacrament, we won't be absolved of our sins. Imagine a priest without holy orders or a married couple without matrimony. We can die a holy death, but how much more so with the anointing of the sick? Only baptism cleanses our souls of original sin and only confirmation fortifies us as soldiers of Christ. We can try to substitute for the sacraments, but the results are never as great as when we follow the original recipe.

Thank goodness the consequences for culinary substituting aren't as severe as sacramental substituting, because I'm not about to change my ways. I enjoy having the kids come in, sniff that pot and ask, "Did you substitute?" When they do, I just smile and let them find out for themselves.

## What does Scripture say?

*So they said to him, "What sign are you going to give us then, so that we may see it and believe you? What work are you performing? Our ancestors ate the manna in the wilderness; as it is written, 'He gave them bread from heaven to eat.'" Then Jesus said to them, "Very truly, I tell you, it was not Moses who gave you the bread from heaven, but it is my Father who gives you the true bread from heaven. For the bread of God is that which comes down from heaven and gives life to the world." They said to him, "Sir, give us this bread always."*

JOHN 6:30–34

## What does my heart say?

▮ How important are the sacraments to me?
▮ Do I ever find myself substituting for the sacraments? How?
▮ How do I substitute for other aspects of my spirituality?

■ ■ ■ ■
# Bumpy Trails and Fading Daisies

I HOPPED ON my clunky old ten-speed bike and took to the trail along Lake Michigan—a very important place for me. All summer long, I'd worked my way up and down that shore either on foot or behind a set of ramhorn handlebars. As my legs and feet worked, my heart and mind worked. I went there to question, sort, grieve, rejoice, reminisce, release, and to just listen to whatever God was saying to me.

It was especially great when the daisies were blooming. Either side of the path became a sea of feathery white petals and bright yellow centers. Daisies are awesome because they're composite flowers. What we consider the "flower" when we look at them is actually a beautiful mosaic of many flowers put together. The more we look, the more we discover about them.

Daisies are like the heavenly Father's plan for me. I think I see the whole beautiful thing in one glance, but when I look closer, I discover a majestic, intricate pattern of tiny flower after tiny flower. I'd spent a lot of time over the past few months meditating on that and contemplating the various components of my daisy-life.

That fall night, I felt a little sad. The flora of summer had already turned into dry brown skeletons and fading grasses. On top of that, the ride seemed bumpier than it had ever been. I cringed as I approached the section across from the seminary, where the path is exceptionally cracked and creviced. I started grumbling to myself and wallowing in self-pity.

"Can't they repave this dumb path? Don't they know how much this hurts? What do our taxes pay for, anyway? This is the worst it's ever been!"

Then I broke out laughing. The *trail* hadn't changed; *I* had! My hours on the trail had worn down some of the...err...cush that used to soften the ride. Those painful bumps symbolized the questioning, sorting, grieving, rejoicing, reminiscing, and releasing I'd done during the summer.

As I made my way toward home, I saw the scraggly brown stalks in a different light. Now they represented all the difficult working-through that I'd endured and the way I'd grown in the process. They have to pass away in order to make room for the mosaic blooms of next summer. Still, I wished I could find just one last, lingering daisy.

Then I saw it—one last bunch of miniature daisies at the edge of the grass. Jubilantly, I waddled the bike over to the plant, reached down, plucked a sprig, and carefully placed it into my pack. I glanced at my watch and panicked. It had gotten late and I had someplace to be! In my rush, I didn't notice that I had knocked the bike out of gear and misaligned the chain. I jumped down on the pedal to give myself a vigorous push-start. Instead of bolting forward, the bike flipped over with me tangled up inside of it.

Thud. I sat there for a moment in stunned silence waiting for my entire body to crumble into millions of pieces like the villains in the cartoons when they whack into a brick wall. Then I broke out laughing again. It hurt like crazy and I was thankful that it did.

That pain was a message from the heavenly Father. The trail can be excruciatingly rugged at times. It can feel like danger lurks around every corner. It can be terrifying to surrender to the twists, turns, and bumps, never certain where I'll end up next. Once in a while I hit the pavement and feel like I'm about to crumble into a million pieces. Sometimes I wonder if I'll meet my demise before I'm able to make it back home.

Then I have to think again of the daisies. Not only must I take in their initial beauty, but also I have to examine them more closely so that I can discover the tiny flower after tiny flower within them. When they fade away, new and even more beautiful ones will bloom. And in the interim, I'll have been remarkably, God willingly, changed.

## What does Scripture say?

*Therefore my heart is glad, and my soul rejoices;*
*my body also rests secure.*
*For you do not give me up to Sheol,*
*or let your faithful one see the Pit.*
*You show me the path of life.*
*In your presence there is fullness of joy;*
*in your right hand are pleasures forevermore.*

Psalm 16:9–11

## What does my heart say?

❙ When has my trail been at its most rugged?
❙ What made it so painful?
❙ How was I changed?

■ ❙ ❙ ■

# Wake Up Call

FOR MONTHS, I've been in a downward spiral of going to bed really, really late and getting up late in the morning. That wouldn't be so bad if I weren't such a slow waker and the mom of a busy family! My family's schedule has been affected by my slipping, too.

A Sunday or two ago, our pastor gave a thought provoking homily on sloth and the ease with which we can slip into this mortal sin. We don't have to be lazy as such, he told us. We just have to succumb to the devil's temptation to do things other than what we're supposed to be doing at the moment as dictated by our vocation.

I wondered if the devil could be using my slipped schedule as a ploy to pull me away from my order of being as a wife, mom, writer, and mentor so I couldn't tackle the good works the heavenly Father has given me. He seems to have more fortune tempting me away from doing good than tempting me to do evil!

Last night before bed, I talked to the Blessed Mother about this. I decided to get to bed at a reasonable hour and then force myself to get up early. I was determined to finish up the article that's due today and be spry and ready for the day (perhaps after several cups of coffee...) by the time the kids got up this morning. "Blessed Mother, you know how weak I am," I pleaded. "I can't do this on my own. You have to wake me up tomorrow and get me going. You're stronger than Satan. Protect me from his cunning."

The alarm went off at 5:00 AM. I groaned and regretted my pleadings of the previous night. I stumbled over to my alarm clock and hit the snooze button. "Nine more minutes in bed won't hurt. It'll help me be less groggy," I told myself.

I snuggled back under the covers and peacefully closed my eyes. The doorbell rang. Our wireless doorbell often goes off for no reason. I tried to ignore it. Then I remembered that Matthew had been working the night before and might be locked out. I hauled myself out of bed and checked his room.

He was sound asleep in bed. I looked out the window. The street was empty.

Then it hit me, and I chuckled to myself. The alarm clock didn't work, so the Blessed Mother rang the doorbell to get me up! I went back to my room, hit the reset button on the alarm clock and joyfully started my day.

They say that lightning can't strike twice in the same place, but the Blessed Mother certainly can. And she did, on the very next night.

I was sound asleep when the doorbell rang. A second later, it rang again. I opened one eye. It was dark outside. "Oh, come on!" I grumbled. "You've gotta be kidding. The alarm hasn't even gone off yet. Doesn't she know when to quit?" I asked myself, feeling sluggish, tired, and at the end of my rope.

Chastising myself for having said my wake up prayer to the Blessed Mother for a second night in a row, I slowly rolled out of bed and fumbled in the dark for the bedroom door. I was amazed at how unbelievably dragged out I was after having slept the night through. How could this be? Was I coming down with something?

I made my way to the top of the stairs and saw that the lights were on below. I heard voices and made my way clumsily down the stairs, one cumbersome step at a time.

"What's going on?" I called out.

Mark met me three quarters of the way up the stairs. He had his jacket on and his hands were cold when he took hold of mine.

"Nothing's going on. I was locked out and Matt let me in," he explained. Then with a big smile he said, "No, honey. It's not the Blessed Mother this time—just me."

"Oh," I said sleepily, not sure if I was disappointed or grateful. "That's almost as good, or maybe better, I think." Delighted that it wasn't time to get up yet, I bumped my way back to bed. As I entered the bedroom, I looked at the clock. It was 12:30 AM!

Even though it was a mere coincidence by most people's standards, I believe that the Blessed Mother really did wake me not once, but twice. Is it because I'm exceptional? Not at all. It's because the Blessed Mother is exceptional. She's a true mother in every respect, always interested in even our slightest needs. She'll go to any lengths to convince us of that. All we need to do is listen for the wake up call.

## What does Scripture say?

> *Besides this, you know what time it is, how it is now the moment for you to wake from sleep. For salvation is nearer to us now than when we became believers; the night is far gone, the day is near. Let us then lay aside the works of darkness and put on the armor of light.*

ROMANS 13:11–12

## What does my heart say?

**I** What kind of sleepiness am I in right now?
**I** What kind of wake up call do I need?
**I** How might I respond?

■ ı ı ■

# Berry Nice Blossoms

I WAS SHOPPING at the wholesale club. As I heaved my already-loaded cart around the corner of the aisle, I happened upon an end cap with bins of gorgeous, fragrant flower bouquets. I stopped and sighed at the variety of vibrant, stimulating colors. My eyes were drawn to a particularly cheerful bunch of daisies with brilliant yellow petals and rich, brown centers.

"Oh…" I swooned. "I should get them for the Blessed Mother."

I scooped the bunch out of the bin. Then I reluctantly put them back. "The flowers I gave her last week are a bit old, but they're still good. I shouldn't spend extra money needlessly," I rationalized. "I'll get her new ones next week."

I paused and looked at those inviting yellow and brown faces. They looked right back at me expectantly. "Oh, shoot!" I said as I caved in and propped them up in the corner of the cart. "The Blessed Mother's worth it. Maybe she'll return the gift somehow." I finished filling my cart and headed for the checkout.

"Whew!" I cringed when the total rang up. I couldn't help mentally subtracting the cost of the flowers from the total to see what I would have spent if I'd left the daisies behind. "This is silly," I reprimanded myself. "You're nitpicking. Let's go, woman!" And I rolled the cart toward the exit.

I passed through the exit line. As the cart monitor handed my receipt back to me, he asked, "Care for some strawberries, Ma'am?" A huge cartload of luscious-looking strawberries was parked behind him.

Even though strawberries are a favorite at our house, I said, "No thanks" and went on my way. Then I heard the guy behind me in line ask if they were giving the strawberries away for free.

"Sure are," the worker replied. "Take as many as you want."

My eyebrows shot up. I grinned a gigantic grin, moseyed over to the cart, and picked out two cartons of ripe, juicy strawberries. On my way out, I did some quick math. The amount I would have paid for the strawberries was twice the amount I had paid for the flowers. The Blessed Mother gave me twice the gift I had given her in return!

Driving home, I thought about those luscious strawberries in the back of the van and felt a little foolish at my stinginess. Our Lady has showered gifts upon me throughout my entire life, and I was hesitant to give her a simple bunch of daisies. She deserves so much more than that. What's wrong with me?

My mind jumped from there to the Blessed Mother's appearance to Saint Catherine Laboure. When our Lady appeared to her in Paris in 1830, Saint Catherine noticed rings on her fingers with stones that sent forth rays of many graces. Some of the stones weren't casting any rays at all, and Saint Catherine asked her about this. The Blessed Mother explained that the stones that don't cast rays represent graces for which no one has asked. The Blessed Mother loves to shower gifts and graces upon her children—she wants all of the stones in her rings to shine.

I want all of the stones in her rings to shine, too. Unfortunately, I sometimes forget to ask for graces or am too stubborn to admit that I need them. Wouldn't it be awesome if I could remember to urge others to ask for her graces? She's waiting for us to do so at this very moment.

That's probably a far better gift than a bunch of daisies, although I'm sure that she enjoys receiving flowers just like any other mom. Giving flowers symbolizes the gift of my heart, and my heart desires all the graces she can give. In return, she gives me the cost of the daisies times two.

### What does Scripture say?

> *But if it is by grace, it is no longer on the basis of works, otherwise grace would no longer be grace.*
>
> ROMANS 11:6

### What does my heart say?

▌ What kind of a gift giver am I?
▌ Do I ever think about giving gifts to the Blessed Mother?
▌ What kinds of gifts could I give her?

■ ❙ ❙ ■

# Chinese Lion Dance

THE DRUMS beat wildly and the cymbals clanged violently. The sound was almost deafening as the lion thrust its gaudy head right into the child's face. I waited for the little one to cry out and scramble away. Instead, she sat placidly in her mother's lap, looking blankly back into the huge, blinking eyes. The security the little girl felt in her mother's care touched me; tears welled in my eyes and a lump grew in my throat.

It was Asiatic Culture Day, and we were witnessing a reenactment of the ancient Chinese Lion Dance at the public museum. The child sitting in her mother's lap was Asian and wore a culturally authentic outfit. However, the child's parents were clearly Caucasian, and I could only assume that this charming little person was adopted.

I marveled at this couple's dedication. I could tell that they were motivated to be there by more than mere curiosity. They obviously wanted to share in the cultural origins of the child God had entrusted to them, to experience more of this wonderful heritage for the child's sake, and to cultivate in her a love for its ancient traditions. With their arms lovingly enfolded around their little girl, they were perfectly at home in this foreign world.

It was hard for me not to stare, because they made me think of the Holy Family. The father fit my image of Saint Joseph—loving, attentive, and kind. The child was serene and unassuming, just as I imagine the Child Jesus. In the mother, I could picture the Blessed Mother holding not only this child, but also every child of every race and nationality throughout the world. I could see her picking each one up, settling each comfortably on her lap, and taking the time to enjoy the culture and characteristics of each one. I could see her looking lovingly into the eyes of each child and into the depths of the soul. Superficial factors can't keep her from being mother to every human being.

Can you picture yourself as a small child sitting in her lap? She's interested in everything about you—your origin, features, culture, needs, preferences, and personality. She's willing to take the time to stop and enjoy with you the things you like to do, to teach you the things you'd like to learn. She worries about whatever you worry about and delights in whatever you take delight. Everything that intrigues you intrigues her. You are her child and she wants to be part of every aspect of your life. With all the people in this wide world, that's an awesome thing to conceptualize.

Yet, it's a reality. What a different world this would be if we all could become so childlike that we could place ourselves in the Blessed Mother's lap and nestle there, serene and unassuming. She would lovingly enfold us in her arms and nothing could disturb our placidity. Nothing at all would alarm us, and we'd never cry out or scramble away—not even when the lion thrusts its gaudy head right into our face.

## What does Scripture say?

*For I know their works and their thoughts, and I am coming to gather all nations and tongues; and they shall come and shall see my glory...*

ISAIAH 66:18

## What does my heart say?

▌ What is the "lion" in my life?

▌ How do I react when he thrusts his gaudy head into my face?

▌ Can I scramble into the Blessed Mother's lap when the lion frightens me? How?

■ ■ ■ ■
# Heart in Heart

I'M FEELING a wee bit jealous. I hadn't anticipated sharing her with anyone except, perhaps, my husband on a limited basis. She's MY little girl, my little princess, and I still hold her on my lap once in a while even though she'll soon surpass my height. Now she's spoiled everything by dedicating herself to the Blessed Virgin Mary. Now she's HER little girl. My only living daughter is under someone else's care.

Really, who am I kidding? Deep down inside me, I know she never really was MY little girl; she's a child of God, and he's given me the astounding privilege of bringing her into the world and nurturing her until she's ready to nurture herself...or someone else.

I learned that the hard way almost eleven years ago while she lay in the neonatal intensive care unit teetering on the edge of death. She'd been born prematurely with an enlarged heart and liver. A few days after birth, she contracted a systemic staph infection that literally took her life and required three tries to resuscitate her. Afterward, she was hooked up to an array of tubes and wires and placed in an isolette. I couldn't hold her. I couldn't even kiss her tender little cheek. The best I could do was to stroke her satiny skin with my fingertips through the vents. When she cried, I couldn't console her. I was a mere bystander, watching the life of my child being weighed in someone else's hands. Inside my mind I screamed, "She's MY little girl, and you can't have her." Inside my heart I sobbed, "Take her if you must."

Those hands—the hands of the heavenly Father—returned her to me, and I've had the last ten years to joke with her, laugh with her, cry with her, sing with her, work with her, play with her, scold her, praise her, and watch her grow into a beautiful young lady both inside and out. For these many years, she's been "mine."

Until now. I watched her kneel in the chapel side by side with the other girls making the same consecration and looking up at the picture of Our Lady with joyful expectation in her eyes. I wanted to run up and shout, "She's MY little girl and you can't have her!" I didn't. She belongs to the Blessed Mother now, and I have to let her go, albeit reluctantly.

I imagine the Blessed Mother understands my selfishness. After all, she was human and felt the same embracing love for her own child. She, too, struggled with watching her child grow up and with having to let go.

To what did she let Jesus go? Three years of living on the streets, traveling, preaching, sustained by the goodness of the earth and the generosity of the people to whom he ministered. After he'd given every bit of himself for the sake of the kingdom of God, they took him into their treacherous hands and fiendishly murdered him. She knows more than the emptiness of letting go!

I thank God that I haven't been asked to make the same sacrifice. Mercifully, I've been given the easy route. I've released Monica into the hands of our loving Mother. She'll hold my little girl's heart next to her own, tenderly coaxing her to the heart of her Son. Monica will be forever shielded in the Blessed Mother's arms, and those arms will offer her far greater protection than I could ever provide.

Inside my heart, I'm joyfully singing, "Take her if you must!"

## What does Scripture say?

> *"For this child I prayed; and the LORD has granted me the petition that I made to him. Therefore I have lent him to the LORD; as long as he lives, he is given to the LORD."*
> *She left him there for the LORD.*
>
> I SAMUEL 1:27–28

## What does my heart say?

∎ What or who am I afraid to entrust to the Lord?
∎ What makes it so difficult for me to let go?
∎ How can I work toward the letting go process?

∎ ∎ ∎ ∎

# Important Things in Life

IF YOU WANT to determine the important things in life, follow a child around for a day. He'll show you all the things that truly count, like examining a bowl of applesauce by smearing it across the high chair tray, his hands, his face, neck, and arms. He'll measure how many toy cars will fit under the couch (fifty-three and still counting at our house…). He'll test the dog's ears to see how far they can be pulled before he gets nipped. He'll experiment to see exactly what floats or sinks in his glass of milk (and then drink it regardless…). He'll figure out just how long a roll of toilet paper is (too long!) by rolling it around the entire house. He'll discover which odds and ends fit in which orifices and at what angle (you don't want to know…). He'll expertly "push my buttons" until I think I'm going to snap, and seconds later melt my heart with his irresistible charm.

A few evenings ago, our family was saying grace at our dining room table. Six-month-old John was seated in his high chair between Mark and me. After we finished praying, we began to serve ourselves but were interrupted by John's exasperated squeals. When I turned to him, he had his hands neatly folded and was hysterically thrusting them up toward my nose.

"Hey, he wants to pray, too," one of the kids called out.

John immediately pulled his little hands in toward his chest and waited. We repeated our meal prayer, this time with John's bright blue eyes roving over our faces, his hands clutched over his protruding tummy. When we were done, John joyfully clapped his hands and began to (literally) dig into his dinner.

John sensed something important in the way we pray together as a family. Now he often drops what he's doing, folds his chubby little hands, and begs someone to pray with him. He's uncovered another one of the important things in life.

One day when John stopped me from working around the house in order to pray with him, I laughingly said to myself, "If the whole world of people stopped, folded their hands, and prayed as often as John does, we'd never get anything done."

Or would we?

Thomas Merton once said, "People who only know how to think about God during fixed periods of the day will never get very far in the spiritual life. In fact, they will not even think of him in the moments they have religiously marked off for 'mental prayer'" (*Seeds of Contemplation*).

Interrupting our activities for prayer seems to hinder us from achieving more, but in reality it's just the power boost we need to shift into overdrive. It's easy to get so wrapped up in our daily work and play that we lose sight of what it was all about in the first place—getting to know God, deepening our love for him, and aspiring to serve him in all things. We can't be reminded of that often enough during the course of our lives.

It doesn't require much effort. There are as many forms of prayer as there are people on this earth. Our prayers throughout the day can be long and formal or brief and relaxed. We can stop for Mass, Scripture reading and reflection, the rosary, or a simple phrase such as, "I love you, Lord" and a promise to offer our next task at hand to his Sacred Heart. In times of stress, sadness, or uncertainty, it can be a "Help me!" sent up to heaven. It's the connection that counts, not the complexity.

What do you suppose would happen if we tried this kind of prayerful reaching out to God for a couple of days? Perhaps it would feel awkward and strained at first. After some practice, we might find that we've discovered the important things in life.

## What does Scripture say?

*Rejoice always, pray without ceasing, give thanks in all circumstances; for this is the will of God in Christ Jesus for you.*

1 THESSALONIANS 5:16–18

## What does my heart say?

❙ With what form or forms of prayer am I most comfortable? Why?

❙ What parts of my day can I use as anchors to remind me to pray?

❙ What form or forms of prayer would I like to learn to practice?

■ ❙ ❙ ■
# Perpetual Helper

IT WAS THE ELEVENTH HOUR, and I was working frantically to meet a deadline. I had one day left to pin down an interview with a Catholic school principal for a story about the new voucher legislation that was recently passed for the Washington, DC, school district. Under normal circumstances, this would have been an easy story to put together. Not this time. The problem was that every single Catholic school principal in the entire archdiocese was attending an all-day seminar and wouldn't return until the following morning. I had to have my article in by morning! What was I going to do?

I decided to wait until the end of the day to call down my list of DC schools to see if by chance any of the principals had gone back to his or her office before going home for the day. I tried Holy Comforter-St. Cyprian and prayed under my breath, "Come on Saint Cyprian, help me out here." No dice. I tried Holy Name and Nativity Catholic Academy. Nothing. It was getting pretty late, and my hopes were sinking. Then I saw it: Our Lady of Perpetual Help. Of course! As I dialed, I begged, "Our Lady of Perpetual Help, I need your help NOW or I'll miss my deadline tomorrow!" Then I held my breath...

The school secretary answered. I asked for the principal. "Oh, she was here, but I think she left," she said apologetically.

" I see," I said disappointedly.

There was a shuffling in the background and then she said, "Wait a minute; could you hold on?" After a long pause, the principal was on the phone, delighted to interview with me. One of the students had caught her just as she was walking toward her car to go home and had relayed my request.

Our Lady of Perpetual Help had answered my prayer!

Within a few minutes, the interview was completed, the principal was on her way home, and I was back to my keyboard. As I pounded out sentence after sentence, I shook my head and smiled. I'd always thought of Our Lady of Perpetual Help as the title under which to implore the Blessed Mother when in imminent physical or spiritual danger. Had it not been for the name of the school, I would never have thought to implore her under that title for something as common as a writer's deadline.

The icon of Our Lady of Perpetual Help is quite intriguing. The legend is that the Child Jesus was frightened by a vision of Saints Michael and Gabriele showing him the instruments of the passion. Jesus fled to his mother for comfort, nearly losing his sandal on the way. She scooped him up in her arms and he placed his hands—palm down—in her hand and apprehensively looked back at the angels.

What I love most is the way Jesus' hands are placed into his mother's. To me, it appears to be a pleading, helpless gesture. I can certainly relate to that feeling of frightful powerlessness! I thought of the most terrifying times in my life, like enduring a cesarean section without effective anesthesia. Like nearly losing an infant from complications of premature birth not once, but three times. Like Mark losing his job after more than two decades of dedicated service to his employer. Like watching Matt go off to war. Like having a madman try to force me off the road by bashing his car into mine. Like facing the lonely depths of my heart when I realize that I've failed my Lord miserably.

During each of those scary, dire times, my perpetual helper was there. Each time, she scooped me up, took me into her lap, and allowed me to rest my hands in hers. She tended to me even during the ordinary snags and irritations of daily life, too, like pressing deadlines and evasive interviews. She was there, perpetually. I implored, and she answered.

## What does Scripture say?

*But you do see! Indeed you note trouble and grief,*
*that you may take it into your hands;*
*the helpless commit themselves to you;*
*you have been the helper of the orphan.*

PSALM 10:14

## What does my heart say?

┃ Who is the first person I run to when I'm really in trouble? Why?
┃ How does that person usually respond to me?
┃ What is it about his/her response that comforts me?

■ ┃ ┃ ■

# My Way or God's Way

I SLAMMED THE BIBLE SHUT, tossed it on the table, and thrust it away from me. I sank back into my chair in disbelief. "That's scary," I thought to myself. I sat there for a long time, numb and motionless, just staring at the Bible. Did God really mean what he said? I shivered slightly and got up the courage to read it again.

It was Psalm 52 which begins, "Why do you boast, O mighty one, of mischief done against the godly? All the day long you are plotting destruction. Your tongue is like a sharp razor, you worker of treachery" (52:1–2).

When I'd grabbed my Bible that morning, I was looking for a message from God. I was distraught over a dilemma in which someone had betrayed me and consequently destroyed something vitally important to me. I was distressed, angry, and fighting the temptation toward revenge. I needed help sorting things out. So I asked God to guide me through Scripture and randomly opened my Bible. I promised to take whatever appeared on the left side of the page as my answer and meditate on it before taking any action.

The next verse was more of the same. "You love evil more that good, and lying more than speaking the truth. You love all words that devour, O deceitful tongue" (52:3–4).

"Exactly," I said to myself. I was relieved to find that the Lord understood my situation perfectly.

Then the psalmist described God's consequences for those who deceive. "But God will break you down forever; he will snatch and tear you from your tent; he will uproot you from the land of the living. The righteous will see, and fear, and will laugh at the evildoer, saying, 'See the one who would not take refuge in God, but trusted in abundant riches, and sought refuge in wealth" (52:5–7).

"Oh, man," I thought to myself. "God doesn't mess around with people like that, does he? That's more drastic than I would have done myself!"

Then it hit me. This whole thing isn't so much about how I think I've been wronged or how I'd like to strike back as it is about letting God be the judge and levy the sentence. God is truth and justice. He sees all, even that which is done in the dark of night. Nothing slips by him and nothing escapes his omnipotence.

The end of the psalm took my meditation in a different direction. "But I am like a green olive tree in the house of God. I trust in the steadfast love of God for ever and ever. I will thank you for ever, because of what you have done. In the presence of the faithful I will proclaim your name, for it is good" (52:8–9).

The olive tree grows slowly and deliberately, constantly reaching toward the heavens and putting all its energy into bearing fruit. It remains unperturbed by its neighbors and surroundings. Any damage inflicted upon it is left to God's tender care and healing. Its sustenance comes directly from him. It's totally dependent on God's goodness.

That's called divine providence. We take in what God sends us through others, through our surroundings, through circumstances, through our inner selves, and allow him to guide us.. It's not about deciding what we want—or what we *think* God should want for us— and then manipulating people and situations in order to achieve it. It's not about knee-jerk reactions and striking back or crushing someone in order to get our own way. It's about being the olive tree that grows slowly and deliberately, constantly reaching toward the heavens and putting all its energy into bearing fruit, and allowing those around us to bear fruit, also.

When I picked up the Bible that day, I wanted an explanation and justification for retaliation. I wanted to know what God wanted *me* to do about it. Instead, God used his word to shake me up and get me thinking in another direction. He let me know what *he* has the power to do about it. In the meantime, my mission is to keep growing, bearing fruit, and trusting in his steadfast love forever and ever.

## What does Scripture say?

> But I am like a green olive tree
> in the house of God.
> I trust in the steadfast love of God
> for ever and ever.
> I will thank you for ever,
> because of what you have done.
> In the presence of the faithful
> I will proclaim your name, for it is good.

PSALM 52:8–9

## What does my heart say?

- ▮ When have I felt betrayed?
- ▮ How did I react?
- ▮ Using the analogy of the olive tree, what are the "fruits" that I bear?

∎ ❙ ❙ ∎

# God's Brave Little Soldier

HE STOOD THERE, his hands buried in our pediatrician's hands, looking directly into his eyes. "Listen, buddy," the doctor said. "We know why you've been feeling so yucky lately—why you're always thirsty and tired. You've got diabetes. That means you're going to be like your mom from now on. You'll need shots and blood tests just like she does. Okay?"

Luke stood there, just staring at the doctor. Then his eyes reddened and began to tear. "Are you okay with that?" the doctor asked as he squeezed Luke's hands. Luke nodded and turned his head away for a second. When he turned back, his eyes were dry, and he nodded again. Then he let go and went to play with the toys in the waiting room.

To me, Luke's reaction was phenomenal. I couldn't believe it. No tantrums. No questions. No complaints. Not an ounce of self-pity or anger. Only acceptance.

On the way home from the doctor's office, I asked Luke if he felt like crying about his unpleasant news.

"Well, only a little," he said. "But that's b'cuz I thought I would have to go and stay at the hospital and that would be so hard for everybody."

Hard for "everybody"? What about being hard for Luke? Since the day he was diagnosed, he has never balked at his condition. He reminds *me* when it's time for each of his four daily finger pokes to test his blood glucose level. He even tests on his own at odd times when he thinks his level isn't right. He calls his twice-daily injections of insulin and the rotation of sites "War Games." His arms are the army, and he watches with scrutiny as I try to shoot down each of the six soldier/injection sights on each arm. His thighs are the navy, with their own sets of six warships each to be attacked. And I'll let you guess for yourself where his air force is. He writes down his own times, blood test results, and insulin doses in his logbook. He's got his meal plan practically memorized.

If this sounds like a tribute to my son, it is. For thirty years, I've struggled to accept my own diabetes. I've griped at the hassle of taking my injections. I've grumbled at the nuisance of having to stop the rhythm of my day for blood tests. And God knows how I complain about having to eat when I don't feel like it and not eat when I'm ravenous. Now I see my little "Cooter," as we've nicknamed him, step along beside me and carry my same heavy cross as if it weighed an ounce.

A few days after that fateful day at the pediatrician's office, Luke came to me and said, "Mom, I know why we're diabetics. It's not our fault. It's nobody's fault. We just are. But I think we are because God wants us to be able to get to heaven easier."

Our family often has talked about sacrifice and the important role it plays in the strength and salvation of not only our family, but of the entire world. We've discussed the mission of the Church to save souls and how we can be more valiant soldiers of Christ. I thought we were preparing the kids for the future. I had no idea we were bracing them for the present.

With childlike simplicity, Luke has embraced his cross. He's resigned himself to the fact that God has asked us to live in this imperfect world. More, he's challenged himself to make the best of a lifelong hardship.

How many of us could emulate his courage and complacency under similar circumstances? How many of us can take up our crosses with such calm readiness? How many of us, in sincere and unquestioning obedience, gaze daily into our crucified Savior's eyes and say, "Yes, Lord. I will do this for you and for the sake of all souls?"

This morning, after our insulin injections, Luke hugged me and said, "I feel bad for you, Mom, b'cuz you have to take so much more insulin than me and have more shots than me." Now Luke and I both have our crosses to carry up the hill. I only hope that someday I'll be strong enough to catch up with him.

## What does Scripture say?

*Share in suffering like a good soldier of Christ Jesus. No one serving in the army gets entangled in everyday affairs; the soldier's aim is to please the enlisting officer.*

2 TIMOTHY 2:3–4

## What does my heart say?

- ∎ In what way has Christ Jesus enlisted me?
- ∎ What battles do I have to fight?
- ∎ How do I approach my "share of suffering"?

∎ ∎ ∎ ∎

# Barefoot Knight

I WAVERED BACK AND FORTH trying to decide whether I should go to an event that night. On the one hand, I had a good reason to go. On the other hand, I just didn't feel like it. I finally decided to pawn the decision off on the Blessed Mother. I told her that if she didn't want me to go, she should do something to stop me in my tracks. Otherwise, I'd take it as a sign that I should go. Nothing prohibitive occurred the whole day long, and so I got ready to go at the last minute.

Monica and I rushed out the door, jumped into the van, and took off. We'd had the van for just a few days, and it was great to have a family vehicle again after several months without one.

A few blocks from home, I heard a weird sound coming from the back of the van. "Do you hear that?" I asked Monica. "What is it?"

"You'd better pull over, Mom," she said. "I think it's a flat tire."

"Well, I guess the Blessed Mother doesn't want me to go after all," I sighed as I eased the van to the side of the road and hit the hazard button.

We got out and went around to the back of the van. It *was* a flat tire. I shook my head, opened the back hatch, and started looking for the car jack and spare tire. Since this van was completely different from our other one, I wasn't sure how to go about changing the tire.

"Better call Dad," I told Monica. "We're going to need some help."

I'd barely had time to pull open the jack compartment when a mid-sized pickup truck pulled over in front of the van and a barefoot, kind-faced young man climbed out.

"Don't worry! I've got it!" he said enthusiastically. "We had a van just like this and ended up on the side of the highway for over half an hour trying to figure it out before someone finally came and showed us how to get the jack and spare out. I know how it goes. Let me do it for you." And with that, he went right to work as Monica and I stood there, stunned.

He crouched down to jack up the van, leaned back, and frowned. "You know what?" he said. "This jack isn't so great. I've got a better one in the back of my truck." He ran back to his truck, pulled out a fairly impressive piece of equipment, jammed it under the van, and got right back to work.

By the time Mark arrived, our barefoot knight had nearly finished the job. Within minutes, the flat was replaced. Once he was sure we were all set, he gave Mark a quick handshake, wished us all a nice evening and vanished.

There was still time to get to the event, so Mark suggested that we switch vehicles and be on our way. As we headed toward Mark's wagon, Monica looked at me with a sly grin and said, "Okay. How far did you get into your 'I Trust Your Mights' before that guy pulled up?" She was referring to my custom of saying three prayers of confidence—one for each member of the Trinity—to Our Lady whenever I'm in desperate need.

"Uh, to tell you the truth," I said sheepishly, "I hadn't even started yet."

"Argh!" she teased. "You don't even have to pray and you get what you want!"

I thought about her comment for a long time after that. For me, the point isn't so much whether or not I had time to pray before our rescuer showed up. What impacted me most was this: No matter what troubles us, no matter what dilemma we face, God always has a better car jack than we do!

## What does Scripture say?

*In you, O LORD, I seek refuge;*
*do not let me ever be put to shame;*
*in your righteousness deliver me.*
*Incline your ear to me;*
*rescue me speedily.*
*Be a rock of refuge for me,*
*a strong fortress to save me.*

PSALM 31:1–2

## What does my heart say?

- When in my life have I been rescued by a "barefoot knight"?
- What was the "car jack" that I intended to use?
- What was the "car jack" that God actually used?

■ **I** **I** ■
# Fresh Air

I'VE BEEN POWER WALKING on the path along Lake Michigan in order to shape up and release stress. It's taken some gumption over the past few months, but now I can push this forty-something body full steam for more than an hour and still make it back home before collapsing. I usually take our standard poodle, Schatzie, along and sometimes a kid or two. Occasionally, I'm blessed to go with Mark when he doesn't have to work late. It's one of my favorite places to be. Once I start tooling down that path with my CD player pumping something upbeat and inspiring into my ears, my troubles and woes melt away and I become a new person.

One evening, it was just the pooch and me clipping along at a pretty sparky pace, and I was feeling really good about myself. There I was, moving down the path, smiling at passersby, head up and breathing deeply—high on adrenaline and God's cool, fresh air. I felt as though I had the world (literally) at my feet.

Suddenly, I breathed in something that was absolutely sinister. Originally, it seemed like an accentuated floral smell, and I thought I'd come into a pocket of newly bloomed wildflowers. But then it took on chemical undertones, seared my nostrils, and started burning my lungs. This certainly wasn't a fragrant product of God's creation that I'd inhaled. I went from glazing and gliding to gasping and gagging in about thirty seconds. My entire body revolted against it; my eyes watered and I became badly congested.

"What in the world happened to God's cool, fresh air?" I asked myself as I tried to work it out of my lungs and nostrils.

It seemed to take forever to clear up enough to continue, but I finally managed. By this time it was getting dark and I needed to head for home. Not wanting to repeat the spectacle, I decided to outsmart the villain and take the other side of the path's loop on the way home. Wouldn't you know it? The same thing happened on the opposite side! Once again I was enveloped in a choking cloud of who-knows-what.

Isn't that how God works in our lives? Sometimes we're clipping along at a sparky pace, thinking we're in great shape and on top of the world. Then suddenly we're gasping and gagging over something absolutely sinister. Sometimes it even happens twice in a row—or maybe more.

The worst part is not seeing it coming. There's no forewarning and we're often aware of it only after it's too late to avoid it. The disgusting vapor we choke on can be any number of things in disguise: pride, ambition, ignorance, betrayal, human frailty, misunderstandings, selfishness, or even demonic influence. It could be that we're on a speedy jaunt in the wrong direction and God needs to stop us in our tracks and set us on the right course. Likely, we'd be too lost in our own power walking to notice a subtle hint from God to pause and redirect.

Is it pleasant? Absolutely not. Is it necessary? Absolutely. Regardless of the cause, every waft of nastiness is a gift from God meant to help us in our personal and spiritual formation. It's not so easy to believe when your eyes are watering, your nostrils are seared, your lungs are burning, and you're so congested that you can barely take a breath. Yet that's exactly the kind of faith we're called to as Catholics. Suffering, humiliation, and confusion mustn't shake us. Each time God stops us in our tracks, he's sending us a message to clear out the sinister stuff from our lungs and nostrils and start again so that we can be stronger in the long run.

No matter how many times we're thrown into a fit of gasping and gagging, we have to clear it out and move on so we can again breathe in God's cool, fresh air. Then we'll be back to glazing and gliding along the path.

## What does Scripture say?

> … when no plant of the field was yet in the earth and no herb of the field had yet sprung up—for the LORD God had not caused it to rain upon the earth, and there was no one to till the ground; but a stream would rise from the earth, and water the whole face of the ground—then the LORD God formed man from the dust of the ground, and breathed into his nostrils the breath of life; and the man became a living being.
>
> GENESIS 2:5–7

## What does my heart say?

- What is "God's cool, fresh air" for me?
- What are the "chemical undertones" in my life that make me gasp and gag?
- How can I clear them out of my lungs and nostrils?

❚ ❙ ❙ ❚

# Living Among Saints

JOHN'S PREMATURE and near-fatal entry into the world and subsequent four-week stay in the neonatal intensive care unit was the most crushing and painful cross our family has had to carry up to this point in our lives. Yet, for as heavy as the cross was, we didn't have to carry it alone.

Because of that experience, I've had the privilege of living among saints. None of them had halos or holy, gaunt faces like we sometimes picture the saints of old. They weren't wearing sandals and long robes, either. Actually, they were pretty modern and ordinary looking. But they're saints, nonetheless.

Throughout the experience, I continually found myself saying not, "Yes, Father" as I know I should, but "Why, Father?" like a stubborn child. However, the one thing I've never had to ask him is "How, Father?" The "how" was shown to me daily through the everyday saints with whom I live.

After John was born, my life became a parade of saints who brought me spiritual fortification and emotional support. I was astounded by the selflessness of the little saints marching around our house. During most of the pregnancy, our ten-year-old Matthew frequently made wonderful breakfasts, lunches, and even dinners for the family just so I could rest. It seemed that every time I turned around, he was there asking if there was anything he could do for me. Our seven-year-old Monica kept my pockets, desk drawers, books, purse, and nightstand filled with "I love you" notes. She (almost) never tired of helping with chores and entertaining her little brother. And five-year-old Luke? He never once complained about being endlessly shuffled from relative to friend to relative while I myself was hospitalized or visiting John in the hospital. During the painful cesarean section and uncertainty of our baby's condition, I gazed into Mark's eyes and squeezed his hand until my blood ran cold. As always, he was right there for me, true as a saint can be.

There are so many more saints who have helped carry us along! John's godparents, in addition to daily prayers and sacrifices, watched a dream of their own vaporize and offered it all up for him. When our family was sick with a virus and couldn't visit John, his kind grandmother put her own important affairs aside and visited him in our stead. Other loved ones cared for our children when we were needed at the hospital and kept our freezer filled with homemade meals and treats. My sadness was lifted when I received a call or letter from a friend who was just checking in to see how we were doing. There's a plentitude of everyday saints who prayed night and day for the success of the pregnancy and later, for John's survival. Many of them I know personally, but some of them I've never met.

I once read that God allows suffering so that humanity might learn to be more compassionate. Our suffering brought forth an outpouring of compassion. Even though I'd do it again in a flash just for the sake of the little person who so blesses our lives, I wish that no one would have to endure what our family has endured. However, I'm certain that if anyone should be asked to carry such a heavy cross, there will be another meshing of heaven and earth with a parade of saints to help ease the weight. I know. I've been privileged to live among the saints.

## What does Scripture say?

*May you be made strong with all the strength that comes from his glorious power, and may you be prepared to endure everything with patience, while joyfully giving thanks to the Father, who has enabled you to share in the inheritance of the saints in the light.*

COLOSSIANS 1:12

## What does my heart say?

**I** What is the heaviest cross I've had to carry?
**I** Who are the saints God sent to help me to carry it?
**I** How did they help me?

▮ ▮ ▮ ▮

# Light as a Feather

YESTERDAY, my intention for holy Mass was to receive an in-break of the Holy Spirit. I wanted to be completely open to all his gifts and fruits and take them deeply into my soul so that I could use them according to God's will. I'd been neglecting the Spirit lately and needed to get back in touch with him.

As I was kneeling there before Mass, I focused on the crucifix. I thought about Jesus' promise to the apostles that he would send the Counselor to comfort and guide them after he'd returned to the Father. Jesus' promise is extended to all Christians, and that includes me. Considering the number of times during my life that I've floundered in my faith, I felt quite pathetic and needy in terms of the Spirit's gifts.

"Holy Spirit," I prayed. "I need you. I've been neglecting you lately and I'm really sorry. Please come to me and fill my heart and soul with your gifts and graces."

My concentration was broken when the entrance procession began and the congregation stood. A few bars into the hymn, something on the floor under the pew in front of me caught my eye.

"No way," I thought to myself. "It can't be."

I leaned forward a little to get a better look. It certainly was. There lay a downy, white feather. It seemed as though the Holy Spirit had come—literally!

It started with a tiny giggle, but I couldn't contain it. Gradually it built up to a laughter I could barely squelch. I'm sure my kids thought I'd finally lost my mind and were making mental preparations to put me away for good this time. I have no idea what Mark was thinking. I'd bring things down to a slow simmer, but whenever the feather caught my eye—which was frequently throughout the liturgy—the giggles bubbled up anew. My shoulders would shake and I'd have to drop my head to my chest so no one could see my face. I imagine the folks sitting around us assumed I was being sacrilegious. In reality, I was marveling at the Holy Spirit's magnificent sense of humor.

As the last note of the recessional hymn faded, I got up, intending to move into the pew in front of me and grab the feather. I wanted to take it home so I could keep it as a remembrance of this unusual encounter with the Holy Spirit. Then I changed my mind. Perhaps another person seeking the Holy Spirit would come along and kneel in this pew and see the feather. Wouldn't it be great to let someone else have the same experience I had just had?

A rationally-minded person could find any number of logical reasons for the feather's presence. It could have floated in the window. It could have fallen off a piece of clothing. But a spiritually-minded person would understand that God can and frequently does speak through ordinary, everyday occurrences. I'm one of the latter. Even if the feather entered the church through ordinary means, the fact that it was there at that moment in time as I was kneeling and praying for that particular intention held an extraordinary message for me.

I left the church thanking the Holy Spirit for humoring me with such a beautiful symbol of his presence. I prayed that I'd never neglect him again and would be reminded often of the feather. I asked for the grace to be continuously open to his mysterious stirrings, even when it's something as light as a feather.

## What does Scripture say?

*"I have said these things to you while I am still with you. But the Advocate, the Holy Spirit, whom the Father will send in my name, will teach you everything, and remind you of all that I have said to you."*

JOHN 14:25–26

## What does my heart say?

- **I** How do I know when the Holy Spirit is at work in me?
- **I** What are the signs of his power within me?
- **I** How might the Holy Spirit speak to me through those experiences?

■ I I ■
# Who's in Control, Anyway?

MARK AND I are taking care of Matt's car while he's serving in the Middle East with the Wisconsin Army National Guard. This morning, Mark took Matt's car in for repairs and asked me to follow a few minutes later so I could give him a ride back home after he'd dropped it off. Since we use two different mechanics—depending on what problem and which vehicle—the shop at which we had the van repaired last week was uppermost in my mind.

Racing out the door, I headed for the repair shop, pulled up outside the front door, and waited. And waited. Then I waited a little more. I looked around the parking lot but didn't see Matt's car.

"That's odd," I thought to myself. Getting a little impatient, I called Mark on his cell phone. "Where are you?" I snapped. "I've been waiting here."

"Where did you go?" he asked.

"I'm over here on Packard," I shot back.

"I'm at the other shop," he replied in his wonderful calm way.

"Arrgh! Hang on, I'll be right there," I said.

As I pulled out of the lot, I grumbled to the heavenly Father and insisted on knowing why he had "messed" with my time at the start of a far-too-busy day. After all, isn't he the one who gave me all these responsibilities in the first place? I've got a family to care for, a household to run, deadlines to meet, other people who depend on me…I haven't got time for this nonsense.

Just after I pulled onto Packard Avenue, I heard a weird sound— almost like slush violently hitting the bottom of the van. Since it was snowing pretty hard, I figured that was the problem. Then suddenly the van was filled with a choking, burning smell, the warning lights on the dashboard went on, and I lost both steering and brakes. Miraculously, I was able to maneuver the steering wheel enough to get the van to the side of the road and coast until it stopped on its own. I threw it into park and turned off the ignition.

My head fell back on the headrest and I heaved a huge sigh of relief. Had the heavenly Father not sent me to the "wrong" shop this morning, I would have taken the route to the other service station and could have lost control of the van on a much busier street, in the middle of an intersection, or even on the highway! Instead of cursing him for wasting my time, I thanked him for sparing me serious injury or an uncomfortable death. In the broad scope of things, "wasting" a few minutes was nothing compared to the trauma a car crash could have caused my family.

This made me think about what time really is after all. I can't contain or expand it. I don't manufacture or control it. The omnipotent One does. He creates time and gives it to me as a gift; it's up to me to be a wise steward and to use it to the best of my capabilities and according to his plan. The idea of spending or wasting my time on something is preposterous, for there would be no time if God did not will it.

Later that night, I reflected on the events of the day. In spite of the van mishap, I was able to get done what was most necessary that day. In the interim, I was saved from a potential tragedy. This was a good reminder to me that my time isn't my own at all. It belongs to our heavenly Father, who knows far better than I do which shop to go to.

## What does Scripture say?

*I have seen the business that God has given to everyone to be busy with. He has made everything suitable for its time; moreover he has put a sense of past and future into their minds, yet they cannot find out what God has done from the beginning to the end.*

ECCLESIASTES 3:10–11

## What does my heart say?

- **I** How do I deal with disruptions to the flow of my day?
- **I** How do I prioritize my time?
- **I** What can I do during the course of my day to remind myself that my time isn't really my own?

■ ▮ ▮ ■

# Where Could That Boy BE?!

IN JEST THE OTHER DAY, I told one of my friends that I liked it better when our two-year-old John was a sickly infant. At least then I knew exactly where he was and what he was up to. It might seem cruel for a mother to say, but anyone who has ever spent more than thirty seconds with a toddler will understand. They never stay in one place longer than a breath and constantly seek new thresholds of danger.

The other day we were at a home-schooling event held at the Schoenstatt International Retreat Center. I was standing in the dining room talking with another mom, and John was standing by my side—or so I thought. In the blink of an eye, he was gone. I searched everywhere for him, but to no avail. As I made my way around hallway and pew, I envisioned what might happen to him if I didn't find him fast. He could unravel the rolls of toilet paper in the restrooms like he does at home. Well, I could replace those. He could destroy all the precious mementos on display. Yikes! I couldn't replace those. He could sneak into someone's office and befuddle the computers. Goodness! I'd have to mortgage my house to replace those. He could burst in on someone's private meeting and scream "Peek-a-boo!" with his uproarious laugh. There's nothing I could do to fix that. Or worse, he might make his way outside and get lost only to be dredged up from the bottom of the lake long after dark that evening. Oh, heavens. I could never replace my little John-John. Where could that boy BE?!

Suddenly, I heard an angelic voice. Was it a messenger from God? Not quite. It was the squeaky little voice of a two-year-old determined to gain entrance to a forbidden space. "OOO-pin! OOO-pin! OOO-pin!" the voice kept squeaking. Then I saw him. He had climbed up to the third floor and was desperately trying to get the door handle of the priest's room to cooperate with his chunky little hands.

It took quite a bit of coaxing to get John to surrender his post. First, I had to convince him not to try to wriggle away from me, lest he wriggle himself under the railing and end up two stories down on the hard tile floor. Once I had his hand trustingly in mine, I had to make certain that he wouldn't try to shake loose and run back up the stairs. I flipped through my entire repertoire of bribes just to find the one that would grab his fancy. Ah! He'd get to help his big brother, Matthew, with the craft project he was working on!

We entered the dining room on a triumphant cloud (at least *I* felt triumphant), and I settled him down next to Matt. *"He's* going to help *me?"* he groaned with raised eyebrows. I patted Matt on the shoulder, heaved a sigh of relief, and went over to check on nine-year-old Monica. As I proudly congratulated myself, I looked up to observe the heartwarming scene of a twelve-year-old head nestled next to a two-year-old head as they collaborated on a work of art.

Wait. I counted just one head.

I hurried over. "Matt, where's John?"

" I dunno, Mom. He just left. I thought he went over by you," he answered.

And the hunt was on again.

As I waited to fall asleep later that night, I thought about how much like toddlers we all are. Determined to seek out new adventures, we slink away from the heavenly Father's grasp. Because we don't fully understand the dangers of escaping his watchful eye, we keep going farther and farther. We try our hardest to gain entrance to those forbidden spaces. The heavenly Father stretches out his arms to us, yet we try to wriggle away, in risk of slipping under the railing. In spite of his beckon, we shake our hand loose and scramble in the opposite direction. We try more and more daring things, until finally we've gotten ourselves into such a predicament that we have nothing left but to cry out, "Abba! Father! Where are you? Come help me!" And, just as I sought John out, the Father seeks us out, coaxing us to place our hand trustingly in his. Then he leads us back to safety. But how long do we remain under his tender care before we wander off on another adventure?

For as many times as we toddle away from him on our stumpy little legs, he lovingly and patiently ensues. No matter how we climb, wriggle, tantrum, or try to shake loose, he is always there. His heart longs to hear us cry, "Abba! Father!" so that he can compassionately scoop us up in his arms, kiss our ouchies, and once again nestle us in the security of his grace and goodness.

And now, if you'll excuse me, there's a little voice somewhere in this house squeaking, "OOO-pin! OOO-pin! OOO-pin!" Where could that boy BE?!

## What does Scripture say?

> *For thus says the Lord God: I myself will search for my sheep, and will seek them out. As shepherds seek out their flocks when they are among their scattered sheep, so I will seek out my sheep. I will rescue them from all the places to which they have been scattered on a day of clouds and thick darkness.*
>
> EZEKIEL 34:11–12

## What does my heart say?

- **I** What causes me to wander?
- **I** Am I usually wandering away from or toward something?
- **I** What is that something?

∎ ∎ ∎ ∎
# Queen of the Office

IT WAS A BUSY Tuesday morning and I was doing the usual—trying to juggle several things at once. I wanted to tend the home, school the kids, and have a project newsletter written up and printed out by the end of the day.

In the middle of dictating Luke's spelling words, overseeing John's history lesson, and feeding paper into the printer for the second-side printing, the paper jammed and the printer went ka-fluey. I'd tried to hurry a new sheet through before the old one had finished printing. Irritated at the delay, I grumbled. Okay. I more than grumbled.

I set the kids in self-study mode (a dangerous thing to do), pulled the printer off its shelf, and pushed the reset button. Nothing. I opened the cover. Nothing. I took the entire printer apart. Nothing. I rebooted it. Nothing. Finally, I spun the printer around and checked the secret trap door in the back. Ahh…. the culprit! Sticking out of the back of the printer were two crumpled faces…not pretty, I assure you. I pried open the back hatch and removed the daring duo along with the rest of the page. Feeling quite self-righteous in my handi-dandiness, I closed up the printer, returned it to its station, and set it back to printing.

Nothing! I gritted my teeth, pulled the printer down again, repeated the entire dismantling procedure, pushed every button I could find, and rebooted it about a thousand times. Nothing, nothing, and more nothing. By this time, more than an hour and a half of my day had been shot and I was rather…well…tense. As I stood, hands on hips, and wondered how one goes about choking a printer (where do you start squeezing?), the Blessed Virgin Mary picture hanging above my desk caught my eye.

I sighed and looked into her eyes. She seemed to be telling me something.

"Aw, come on!" I thought. "You mean to tell me I'm supposed to come to you even with something as basic as a dippy printer?" I shook my head in exasperation. "Fine. Whatever you want, good Mother.

You've been crowned Queen of Heaven and Earth by the Church; you can be Queen of the office here. I've done all I can with this thing. I give up. I'll just sit here and pray until you make yourself victorious and fix my printer."

As I stubbornly lowered myself onto the chair, I felt something beneath me. Standing up, I turned around to see what it was. There on the seat sat the ink cartridge! Feeling myself grow red with embarrassment, I gave the Blessed Mother a sheepish grin, picked up the cartridge, plopped it back into the printer, put the printer back in place and finished printing the newsletter.

She certainly taught me who's Queen of the office!

As Catholics, we're called to believe in Mary's queenship. We celebrate it as a feast day on August twenty-second, and we meditate upon it in the fifth Glorious Mystery of the rosary. Yet I sometimes forget all the implications and responsibilities that title bears.

A queen radiates the dignity and power of her station, while at the same time deferring to the dignity and power of the king. The king in turn protects the dignity and power of the queen, assuring the respect and admiration of her subjects. We're the subjects of the Blessed Virgin Mary and our Lord Jesus Christ. Our King loves and trusts his Queen Mother so much that he grants her the privilege and responsibility of mediating his graces to us. Nothing escapes her concern, not even the small and seemingly insignificant details. She's a queen who never rests, is never distracted, and never leaves our sides. What an awesome reality to absorb!

I'm sure I'll need to be reminded of this in the future; I so often get caught up in my own narrow-mindedness and humanness. I might forget about her power and position, but she won't. That's when I'll find myself sitting down on an ink cartridge again.

## What does Scripture say?

*When your days are fulfilled to go to be with your ancestors, I
will raise up your offspring after you, one of your own sons, and
I will establish his kingdom.*

1 CHRONICLES 17:11

## What does my heart say?

∎ What does the title Queen of Heaven and Earth mean to
me?
∎ I am a child of the kingdom—what does that mean to
me?
∎ What "ink cartridge moments" have I had in my life?

∎ ∎ ∎

# Letting Go

THE NIGHT WAS CHILLY, but I was trembling more from emotion
than from the cool night air. A lump rose in my throat, and I had
to swallow hard to keep it from choking me. Tears began to form at
the corners of my eyes and I bit my lip, trying to hold them back. I
watched in pride as the cadets moved in unison while the lieutenant
barked out the drill commands. My eyes were glued to one of the cadets in the middle row. It was my fifteen-year-old son, Matthew. The
drill demonstration was part of an open house held by Matt's Civil
Air Patrol squadron.

I hadn't expected to be driven to tears just watching a drill demonstration. But seeing him there among the other cadets in uniform,
following the commanding officer's directions drove home a harsh
reality. My son was growing up! The mixture of appreciation and loss
was overwhelming.

Belonging to Civil Air Patrol—a volunteer auxiliary branch of the
United States Air Force—is just one step in his path toward adulthood. Recently he told us he's thinking of joining one of the Armed

Forces. I never dreamed that one of my children would be called to the military. It's a noble, worthy calling, but also one that could mean physical distance and danger.

A few months ago, he got a job at the library, and I'm still trying to get used to seeing him off to work four days a week. Sometimes I call around the house looking for him and then sadly remember that he's at work. It seems like such a short time ago that I was seeing him off to a playmate's house. How did this all come about so quickly?

Sometimes I think that when the heavenly Father structured the stages of life, he forgot about parents like me who aren't in any hurry to see their kids grow up. I don't want them to remain dependent; I simply *like* having them around. They're wonderful, fun people and when they're at home, somehow everything just seems so…right.

Thank goodness God is in charge. He knows the perfect timing for everything. In his wisdom, he knows it's time for me to begin letting go of Matt. Deep in my heart, I know it, too. It's in God's divine plan this way, and it will be in his divine plan when it's time to let go of our other three children in their turn. If I don't let them go, they'll never mature into the responsible adults who, along with their peers, will help to lead the Church into the future.

We all have children who must grow up and leave the nest. It might be a biological, adopted, or foster child, or it might be the persons in our charge, a project, possession, career, apostolate, or dream. These are all things to which we can become inordinately attached, causing us to fight the letting-go process.

Fight as we might, it won't do any good. Jobs change. Routines are disrupted. Good works are derailed. Projects fail. Adversaries conquer. Property is ruined. People move on. The heavenly Father asks us to let go for our own good and the good of the others. He knows that we can only become fully attached to him if we become prudently detached from the people and things around us.

That doesn't mean we should be cold, callused, and forgo all attachments and relationships. We're created in God's image and likeness with a vocation to love. Rather, we should see each thing, each situation, and each person in our lives as a gift from God and an instrument in our own faith journey. In turn, we have to realize that we play the same role in the lives of others and thus instrumentally allow them to follow their own unique path toward sanctity.

I'm not sure when the next Civil Air Patrol open house will be, but I guarantee that I'll be there. I also guarantee that I'll get choked up again. I'll see visions of Matthew as a little boy, zooming down the sidewalk on his bicycle. I'll remember the smell of his hair as he snuggled into my lap for a story. I'll think of the countless pictures he drew for me. I'll thank God for the time I had with him. Then I'll utter a desperate plea for the grace to stand firm in this time of letting go.

## What does Scripture say?

*"Do not let your hearts be troubled. Believe in God, believe also in me. In my Father's house there are many dwelling places. If it were not so, would I have told you that I go to prepare a place for you? And if I go and prepare a place for you, I will come again and will take you to myself, so that where I am, there you may be also."*

JOHN 14:1–3

## What does my heart say?

**I** What does it mean to be ordinately or inordinately attached to someone or something?

**I** To what or whom am I inordinately attached?

**I** To what or whom am I ordinately attached?

**I   I   I**

# Princess Demento

OUR WHITE standard poodle, Schatzie, constantly is the brunt of our ridiculous Fenelon Clan humor. Poor thing: her name itself is a joke. Before we got her six years ago, Mark and I suggested that the kids do a little research about the origins and characteristics of the breed so we'd have some knowledge of how to raise and train her and perhaps a clue as to a name for her.

Internet research turned up lots of great information. Standard poodles were originally German hunting dogs. The fuzzy poufs of fur on their heads and bodies acted as insulation when they dove into cold water to retrieve the spoils of the hunt. Eventually, poodles made their way over to France, where King Louis XV, with his fetish for flare, discovered that their coats could be groomed into all sorts of marvelous and extravagant styles. Thus, they gained the reputation for being prissy French poodles.

Considering our dog's German heritage, we decided to look up a proper German name for her. We found a list of German dog names and considered each one carefully. Based on her gentle temperament, we chose Schatzie, which means "little darling." We were pretty proud of our international poodle and cultural savvy.

However, the joke was on us when a group of German pilgrims came to visit our house. We introduced our family members one by one and then proudly introduced our appropriately named German poodle. Instead of smiling and appreciating our dog's ethnicity, they all broke out laughing. Mark and I looked at each other, dumbfounded.

"Is something wrong?" Mark ventured.

"That's what we call our wives!" one of the men chortled.

Well, we may have been mistaken in the application of Schatzie's name, but we were right on track with the meaning. As the years have gone by, she's become more and more loving and docile. In spite of her heft and gangly legs, she tries at every opportunity to climb into any available lap. She snuggles up to people with a sad, longing look in her eyes that's so pathetic and endearing that you simple have to pet her. And pet her. And pet her, because she'll claw you nearly to death if you stop. She's so meek and gentle that at times she appears to confuse easily, even though she's very smart. That's why we've fondly nicknamed her Princess Demento.

The thing that amazes me most about Princess Demento is her humility and trust. Her favorite place to be petted is on her throat, right over the jugular. She'll sidle up beside me, tip her head all the way back, close her eyes, and wait for me to begin stroking her. The firmer I rub, the more ecstatic she gets. What a credulous and vulnerable thing to do! Canine jests aside, I can't imagine myself in the same place and acting in the same way. It would be a tremendous leap of faith to open my very lifeblood to the hands of another.

Schatzie's relationship with me reminds me of what my relationship with the heavenly Father should be like. No doubt he sees me as more valuable than a dog, but the principle is the same. He wants me to seek his love and attention and come to him in complete humility and trust. He wants to develop a relationship with me that is so intimate that I'll be able to place my lifeblood into his hands with credulous vulnerability.

In return, he gives me his undivided love and attention. With his kind, benevolent hand, he forms me into the creature of his desire— the vision he has had of me from all eternity. In spite of my human "dementia," I'm his favorite child. He has chosen me and wants me to respond to him in holy docility so that he can help me to develop the strength and courage to lay my life before him without fear, without reserve.

We make fun of Princess Demento with her strange mannerisms and seemingly slow wit, but by observing her I've learned a great deal about the way I should interact with the heavenly Father. Perhaps someday my relationship with him will more closely resemble Princess Demento's relationship with me.

## What does Scripture say?

*Blessed are those who trust in the LORD, whose trust is the LORD.
They shall be like a tree planted by water, sending out its roots
by the stream. It shall not fear when heat comes, and its leaves
shall stay green; in the year of drought it is not anxious, and it
does not cease to bear fruit.*

JEREMIAH 17:7–8

## What does my heart say?

▮ Do I feel confident approaching the heavenly Father?
▮ How do I relate to him?
▮ Could I really place my "jugular" into his hands? Why or
why not?

▮ ▮ ▮ ▮

# A Stalled Car and an Angel on a Bike

"OH, DEAR LORD," I prayed. "Please don't do this to me. Not here…
not now."

Sure enough. He *was* doing this to me. The car had stalled out in
the middle of a busy street and in a neighborhood that can be pretty
rough after dark. It was dusk.

A city transit bus pulled up behind me and waited there. I panicked.

"What am I going to do?" I asked no one in particular. Little
John was sitting in the back seat and I told him to get Dad on the cell
phone right away.

In the mean time, I held my breath and panicked even more as
the bus began to squeeze through in the partial lane next to me. It was
so close that all I could see was the white background and the top of
the green stripe along the side as it inched its way past my passenger
window. My head started pounding and my spine went cold.

Amazingly, the bus made it through. But right behind it was a lane of cars with some very unhappy drivers who weren't as daring about squeezing through.

John had Mark on the phone and handed it to me. He was on his way and would be there as soon a he could.

"Not soon enough!" I blurted into the receiver. "I've got a line of cars behind me who are very interested in seeing me move this thing NOW!"

"Okay, I'll hurry. Hang on," he reassured me. I tossed the phone back to John and futilely tried to start the car again.

Then I heard someone shouting.

"Oh, great. Thanks, Lord," I grumbled, certain that it was a disgruntled motorist coming to wring my neck.

I looked up and saw a hip, thirty-something guy on a bike riding down the center island toward me. He was shouting, "You need a push? It's okay. I'll push you."

He laid his bike down in the grass and came toward the car. "Throw it in neutral, and I'm gonna push you into that driveway over there," he said as he pointed about half a block up the street.

By the time he made his way to the back of the car, the other drivers' patience had worn out. There were irritated shouts and horns going off. "Hey!" I'm gonna push her, OKAY? Just take it easy," he shouted defiantly.

Within a couple of minutes, the car was in the driveway. He came around to my window and I heartily thanked him.

"Hey, no problem," he said as he reached in and shook my hand. Then before he left, he said, "God bless you!"

"God bless you, too," I said numbly.

I sighed in relief and sunk back into my seat. Suddenly, he was back.

"Hey, did you call somebody?" he asked. "Somebody's comin' for you, right?"

"Yeah, I called my husband. He's on his way," I replied. "Thanks again."

"Okay then. Just checkin'. Good night." And he was gone.

I was surprised at this man's kindness and disappointed that all I could offer him was a feeble thank you. I wished there was something more I could have done for him. Then I remembered his bike! He had left it lying there. It could have been stolen.

So I prayed, "Please, Lord. Make sure he gets his bike back. Don't let it be stolen. He did something so kind for me; please be kind to him."

I'll never know whether or not he got his bike back. I'll probably never know why our Lord chose to stall the car on that street at that moment. I do know that in the midst of a bleak situation, our Lord showed me that there's always hope. Sometimes it's from the most unexpected source, like an angel on a bike.

### What do Scriptures say?

> "The LORD is my portion," says my soul,
> "therefore I will hope in him."

LAMENTATION 3:24

### What does my heart say?

∎ When have I felt truly hopeless?
∎ Who were the "angels" that brought me hope?
∎ When have I been an angel of hope for someone else?

∎ ∎ ∎ ∎

# See Why

I DON'T OFTEN drive alone, but when I do, I make the most of it. My solitary drive time is important to me, because it's a somewhat automatic activity that frees my mind to rove and meander in indiscriminate directions.

This day, I was sailing down the highway with my mind pitching to and fro over an issue I couldn't understand. Troubling events had unfolded that I felt were unjust, and I wanted to do something about it. Letting it brew in my mind, of course, merely fueled my indignation. But as I drove, prayed, and contemplated, my thinking began to change. God graciously and wisely unraveled my reasoning and brought things into perspective. He showed me that things probably weren't at all as they had originally appeared.

Amazed at these revelations, I praised and thanked the heavenly Father for the way he had urged me to stop and think before jumping to conclusions. Just then, I pulled along the side of a semi on which one word was written in large, simple blue letters. It said, "SEEWHY."

"What's a SEEWHY?" I asked myself. I played with the letters a bit in my head and wondered what kind of a company would name itself SEEWHY or what kind of product a SEEWHY was.

Then I chuckled. "Oh, I get it!" I exclaimed. "Not SEEWHY. It's SEE WHY. Ha! See why things have happened before making hasty judgments!" I laughed for a long time after that. It seemed absurd that those letters ended up on a truck next to me on the highway at that very point in time.

A few days later, I was driving home from a meeting. Again, I was contemplating the same set of events, the lesson God had taught me through them, and the funny message he had sent me on the side of the semi. In a fog of thought, I pulled up at a stoplight and let my eyes come to rest on the license plate of the metallic maroon Ford Taurus sedan one car ahead of mine and in the next lane. My mind was quickly brought into focus and I broke out laughing.

The car's license plate said, "SEEWHY."

Apparently, the heavenly Father thought this lesson was so important that he wanted me to learn it not just once, but twice. It's easy to observe or experience something and then make a snap judgment about its origins and causes. It's so easy to cast out the demons of doubt and suspicion, take everything into account, and carefully search through each detail in order to see why it happened before retaliating. In fact, sometimes it can seem impossible.

I'm reminded of a time when a friend initiated a project and invited me to participate in it. I understood that I was to become a main player in the game; he understood that I was a disposable and temporary player. Unfortunately, we never clearly communicated this to each other. The harder I tried to create a viable position for myself, the more irritated he became with me. The more irritated he became with me, the harder I tried to create a viable position for myself. This continued until the whole thing ended in a hurtful disaster.

If we had stopped to examine the reason things were unraveling the way they were, the calamity could have been avoided entirely. Instead, we focused on our own ambitions and notions rather than opening our hearts and minds to the desires and motivations behind the other's behavior. We simply didn't see why.

I imagine we all have times in our lives when we're flying down the highway and need a semi to pull up along the side of us to remind us to consider things more carefully. In a period of desperate confusion, even a license plate would do. We just have to open our hearts and minds in faith so that the demons can be cast out. Then we'll see why.

## What does Scripture say?

*Then the disciples came to Jesus privately and said, "Why could we not cast it out?" He said to them, "Because of your little faith. For truly I tell you, if you have faith the size of a mustard seed, you will say to this mountain, 'Move from here to there,' and it will move; and nothing will be impossible for you."*

MATTHEW 17:19–21

## What does my heart say?

❙ What was the most confusing time in my life?
❙ What made it so confusing?
❙ Where was the heavenly Father's hand in that situation?

∎  I  I  ∎

# I've Got Bing!

I PICKED UP THE TAG and smiled. It had a caricature of a guy with an Afro hairstyle and a great big diamond earring in his left ear. I was rabble-rousing with a bunch of young people and the tag came from one of the ridiculous neon-colored foam wigs we'd bought from the discount store just for fun.

"Hey!" I called out. "Look! This guy's got bing!"

The others stopped mid-conversation and looked at me.

"He's got what?" one young woman asked.

"He's got bing!" I replied.

"What's that?" she asked.

I was so amazed that I actually knew a hip word that the young crowd didn't know that I squealed in delight. "Ha Ha Ha! I can't believe it! I can't believe I know a hip word you don't know!"

I grabbed the tag and pointed to the large jewel nestled into the figure's earlobe. "Look! Right there! He's got a bing!"

Suddenly the quiet erupted into laughter.

"That's not a *bing*!" the young woman explained. "It's a *bling*!"

My eyes widened, and I felt the glowing red warmth of embarrassment working its way up my neck and toward my face. Then I started laughing, too. I'd heard the term only once before—from a friend who obviously was more hip than I was, and I'd remembered it incorrectly. That's what I get for trying to show off.

Thanks be to God, my hip-haughtiness didn't offend my young cohorts. In fact, it somehow became a means of endearment. Now when we get together, any piece of jewelry becomes a "bing" and anyone wearing more than one item at a time has the right to exclaim, "I've got bing!"

I'm like that with the Word of God sometimes. I hear it with a casual attitude and think I've got it. At a later time and place, I try to pull it out of my "hip pocket" and use it to make an impression. This isn't intentional, of course. I want to hear, understand, and internalize

God's Word. I want to be able to use it accurately so that it makes a good impression on others.

Unfortunately, my human imperfections get in the way. I become distracted and so I don't really hear what God's saying to me. Sometimes I try to concentrate and take it in correctly, but my own biases prohibit me from fully understanding it. At other times, I get it right away but don't take care to practice it so that it becomes a part of my natural dialect. Then when I try to use it, I find I've lost some of the important details.

What a blessing that the heavenly Father is even more forgiving than young adults. He patiently allows me to take in what I can of his Word, knowing that his human child isn't capable of understanding the fullness of his mystery. He waits in the background as I try to use it accurately, because he knows that's the best way for me to learn. Practice makes perfect, and each time I attempt to accept and apply his Word, I get a little better at it.

When I get it wrong, he lovingly sends me a guide to redirect me. Depending on the situation, the redirection can be subtle and lighthearted or distinctive and forceful. It can be a jovial jab in the ribs or a stern slap in the face. Regardless, it's always done in benevolence and wisdom. He speaks his Word to me and listens for me to echo it back to him. Each time I say "bing," he gently corrects me and says, "No, it's bling."

Eventually, I'll get it and be able to say, "I've got bling!"

## What does Scripture say?

*I treasure your word in my heart,*
*so that I may not sin against you.*
*Blessed are you, O LORD;*
*teach me your statutes.*
*With my lips I declare*
*all the ordinances of your mouth.*
*I delight in the way of your decrees*
*as much as in all riches.*

*I will meditate on your precepts,*
*and fix my eyes on your ways.*
*I will delight in your statutes;*
*I will not forget your word.*

*Deal bountifully with your servant,*
*so that I may live and observe your word.*

PSALM 119:11–17

## What does my heart say?

- **I** What importance does God's Word play in my life?
- **I** How does he speak to me?
- **I** How do I listen to him?

■ I I ■

# Who, What, Where, When and How Come?

MY SON is giving me theology lessons. He isn't a theologian. He isn't even a priest or deacon. In fact, he doesn't even have a high school diploma. My son is an insatiably inquisitive four-year-old.

In spite of his young age, he's duped me time and time again. He comes up with questions that are out of this world—literally. He turns the same question round and round until I become so entangled that I'm at a loss for words. It can be truly embarrassing.

The last time I felt this belittled was the time my college professor pounded his fist on the table of the *Milwaukee Journal* computer room and screeched, "Who pushed the button that deleted the entire class's assignments!?" I, of course, knew it was me. And so did he.

I feel that same need to slip under the rug when Matthew approaches me and begins cornering me with questions. "Mommy, if our guardian angels keep us safe all the time, why do we lock our doors at night?" "How do the angels keep the devil away from us? Do they box him?" "If God can do anything, why does he let some people act mean?"

Answering, "That's just the way it is" never works. Something theologically sophisticated would be way over his head and frustrate him. Something too simplistic would only multiply the number of questions and drive me insane. Still, he needs and deserves answers that will satisfy his curiosity and keep him interested in his faith, while at the same time not burdening his young mind with things he shouldn't yet be worrying about.

It seems that's exactly what the heavenly Father does with me. I'm so often like an insatiably inquisitive four-year-old trying to corner God with my out-of-this-world questions. I turn them round and round and try my best to entangle God in them so that he's forced to give me the answers. But he's infinitely more clever than I am and can't be entangled, no matter how hard I try.

Instead, I'm the one who becomes entangled. I want to know the who, what, where, and how come of every detail of my life. I want to know who can help me out of a tight situation. I want to know what can be done about someone who has harmed my reputation. I want to know where we'll find enough income to support our family. I wonder how come something I've put my lifeblood into has been destroyed.

The more I ask and entangle, the worse things become and the farther I get from grasping the heavenly Father's wisdom. He can't give me the information I want; he has to give me the information I need. Something too theologically sophisticated would be way over my head and frustrate me. Something too simplistic would only multiple my questions and drive me insane. The heavenly Father has to give me enough answer to satisfy my curiosity and keep me interested, while at the same time not overburdening me with things I shouldn't be worrying about.

I know just how Matt feels. The world is mystifying, and there's so much to know and understand—so many questions that need answers. We have to ask those questions, because it's part of our human nature. If we don't ask, it means we're not interested. And if we're not interested, we stagnate and our faith will fall away. But we have to learn the childlike trust that will help us to be satisfied with the information the heavenly Father gives us. It'll be just what we need for the time being.

## What does Scripture say?

*"Therefore do not worry, saying, 'What will we eat?' or 'What will we drink?' or 'What will we wear?' For it is the Gentiles who strive for all these things; and indeed your heavenly Father knows that you need all these things. But strive first for the kingdom of God and his righteousness, and all these things will be given to you as well. "So do not worry about tomorrow, for tomorrow will bring worries of its own. Today's trouble is enough for today."*

MATTHEW 6:31–34

## What does my heart say?

❙ What are the questions that most frequently rise within me?

❙ Why do they plague me?

❙ What resources do I have to help me better understand God's ways?

❚ ❘ ❘ ❚
# Author of History

WHENEVER I LISTEN to the news reports about the violence in the Middle East, I can't help but think back to September 11, 2001, when terrorists hijacked three airliners, sending two of them plowing into the World Trade Center towers in New York and slamming the third into the ground in Pennsylvania. I also can't help but remember that's the main reason why Matthew enlisted in the Wisconsin Army National Guard and subsequently spent a God-awful year of deployment in Kuwait. And why he's spending another in Iraq.

Sometimes it enrages me. Sometimes it confuses me. Sometimes it depresses me. Always it scares the dickens out of me. When that happens, I place my hand in the hand of Our Lady, entrust my son, my family, my country, and my world to her, and go back to a piece I wrote shortly after the terrorist attacks…

❚ ❘ ❘ ❚

Walking the dog brings tears to my eyes almost every morning. The neighbors probably think that the dog's pulling too hard at the leash and strangling my hand or I'm suffering from major shin splints. That's not it. It's the rows and rows of American flags I pass as I wind my way through my neighborhood and down to Lake Michigan.

They're everywhere: flanking front doors, guarding winterized gardens, lining walkways, clinging to windows, hitching a ride on passing cars. They're a silent message from their owners, a profession of our country's stand for unity and resolve to never give up. They decry the horrors of a mindset that devalues human life and contorts pure principles into edicts of death and destruction. They stand proud and sing out, "…let freedom reign."

Before September 11, 2001, not nearly as many of these flags would have been hailing me each morning. A few might have decorated the block on Flag Day, the Fourth of July, or Veteran's Day, but the flags would've gone back to the closet at the holiday's end. In the pre-terrorist attack days, there just wasn't the same urgency to display the flag as there is today.

It's become a symbol of our new definition of freedom, formed because of the attacks. It used to mean having what we wanted, where we wanted it, and when we wanted it. Freedom was what we did on the outside in order to feel good on the inside. Our new definition of freedom is affected by the limitations necessarily placed upon us by future terrorist threats, resulting in stronger security measures, and whatever else may be asked of us. Freedom has come to mean what we are on the inside—who we are, what we stand for, what we're willing to endure. The flags that fly throughout our nation represent that.

If anything positive can be derived from the terrorist crisis, it's that we Americans are slowly beginning to realize that God is the source of our freedom. How many times in the past months have we heard the words, "God Bless America"? They show up everywhere: theater marquees, gas station signs, school banners, and bumper stickers to name a few. Even our little five-year-old John goes around the house humming, "God Bless America, because I'm home...." Our helplessness has urged us to rediscover our spirituality.

I took the children to Mass at noon on September 11. It was our usual day to go, but that day we were more eager to go than ever. The church was more filled than normal and everyone seemed to be looking for consolation and answers for the tragedy that had struck our homeland. As the priest lifted the host high in the air for all to adore, a single thought crossed my mind: "No matter what, our Lord is the author of history." I hung on to that thought as though my life depended on it, because it does. In fact, all of our lives depend on it.

As any author, he takes the utmost care to see that his characters become well-rounded. He treats them tenderly, because he created them. He looks after their needs, peers into their futures, and prepares the way for the plot to play out in exactly the right way. America is a free nation, because he authored it so. Everything we have is a product of his goodness. Everything we stand to lose belongs in his hands. Everything we wish to gain must be consecrated to him. As a nation, we're beginning to see that our destiny depends on the way he has allowed his pen to flow over the paper. The flying of the flags and the singing of the anthem echo his words in our hearts.

❙ ❙ ❙

As we ramble up to the back gate—me trying to warm my icy cheeks and the dog making a scratch mark in the dirt for every squirrel she's rattled—I turn around and take one last look at the neighbor's flag. As I do, I'm reminded that our lives are securely in the hands of the author of history, and I faintly hear that robust little voice, "God bless America, because I'm home.…"

## What does Scripture say?

*Now these are the nations that the LORD left to test all those in Israel who had no experience of any war in Canaan (it was only that successive generations of Israelites might know war, to teach those who had no experience of it before)…*

JUDGES 3:1–2

## What does my heart say?

❙ What is the most catastrophic event I've ever witnessed?
❙ How did it affect me?
❙ How can I see the hand of God in that?

■ ▎ ■

# The Golden Catholic

WHAT IF SOMEONE asked you, "What religion are you?" I bet you'd reply, "I'm Catholic." But what would you respond if that same person then asked, "What kind of Catholic?" Perhaps you'd answer, "Roman Catholic" or "Eastern Rite Catholic." Perhaps you'd be stuck, as I was when I asked myself that question.

I consider myself a practicing Roman Catholic. But, what *kind* of practicing Roman Catholic am I?

Not long ago, I read an excerpt from a talk given to a group of priests in the 1930s by Father Joseph Kentenich. In it, he spoke of the iron priest, the silver priest, and the golden priest. The iron priest, Father Kentenich says, is one who does his duty as perfectly as possible and nothing more. He simply wants to do his job and live his private life as he sees fit and isn't motivated by the desire to save souls. The silver priest, however, is concerned with saving souls one hundred percent of the time. This is quite admirable, but his motivation is his own fulfillment rather than the glory of God. In contrast, the golden priest relentlessly cares for souls only to honor God and to save souls. Regardless of the magnitude of the work, he takes it up with love, joy, and confidence in divine providence.

This measure can be applied, not only to priests, but also to all members of the Catholic Church. One might be considered an iron Catholic, a silver Catholic, or a golden Catholic. Therefore, I have to ask myself: "What kind of Catholic am I?"

If I were an iron Catholic, I'd follow the precepts of the Church precisely. I'd say my prayers, receive the sacraments, and basically mind my own business, focusing on the confines of my own four walls. I'd do no harm to my neighbor; nor would I go out of my way to do him any good. At the end of each day, I'd be able to say that I did my duty—no more, no less.

If I were a silver Catholic, I'd follow the Church's precepts, say my prayers, receive the sacraments and constantly seek opportunities to be a good Samaritan. I'd not only help my neighbor, but I'd help strangers just for the thrill of being needed. My reward would be knowing that I'm a good person because I went out of my way to do a kind deed.

Ah, but if I were a golden Catholic, I'd joyfully follow the precepts of the Church (and then some), eagerly and often receive the sacraments, say my prayers with love and deliberation, follow the counsels of the saints, and begin each day by offering every moment of it up for the greater glory of God. I'd make a conscious effort to be open to any and all opportunities through which God could use me as his instrument to save another soul. If I were a golden Catholic, I'd daily realize that my life is not my own, but a gift which I must bring to fruition.

I often feel more like I'm made of iron than gold. I feel heavy, awkward, immobile and inflexible. I'd rather stay comfortable in my private enclosure and let the rest of the world go by. I say my prayers and try to avoid sin, but without any real enthusiasm. I do what is expected of me according to my vocation, but without any extras. My main goal is just to get from one end of the day to the other.

At other times, I feel made not only of silver, but of tarnished silver—hidden under layers of insecurities, imperfections, and helplessness. I seek self-gratification and want only to have others notice my goodness, because it makes me feel more important and less apprehensive. I flit around doing superficial acts of kindness because the pats on the back I receive for them fill a void. I do something charitable because it's nice to be needed and helps me find favor with God.

Trying to be a golden Catholic is much more challenging. It requires a consistent effort that must override my personal thoughts, feelings, and ambitions (or lack thereof). My striving to be a golden Catholic is most fruitful when my entire being is in true harmony. My prayers become a song of inspiration and a living connection between the heavenly Father and myself. My actions become a desire to please him rather than a fear of evil. My vocation becomes a prized work of art—a slow, careful process that will create a thing of lasting beauty. At those times, I'm totally open to God's love, which fills me to overflowing so that I simply must share it with all his children. I beg to be his instrument and avail myself to his every wish and whim in all aspects of my life. It seems as though there aren't enough minutes in the day in which to devotedly do his work.

Whenever I find myself acting as though I'm made of the less-precious metals, I flee to the solace of the Blessed Mother. I find a quiet place and sit quietly, enveloped in her arms. Forcing myself to be brutally honest, I empty myself completely into her immaculate heart. When I've poured out every last fault, complaint, and misgiving, I offer myself to her and ask her to fill me with the grace necessary to become a golden Catholic. In return, she fills me with her tender mother-love, consolation, peace, courage, and the confidence to try anew. With her beside me, I feel capable of anything the heavenly Father asks of me. With her help and guidance, I can become more resolute in my striving. Indeed, she can turn iron into gold.

## What does Scripture say?

*…so that the genuineness of your faith—being more precious than gold that, though perishable, is tested by fire—may be found to result in praise and glory and honor when Jesus Christ is revealed.*

1 PETER 1:7

## What does my heart say?

∎ How do I live my Catholic faith on a daily basis?
∎ In what areas do I most often fail?
∎ What kind of Catholic am I?

∎ ∣ ∣ ∎

# Family Mission

A YOUNG COUPLE visited us the other night. We had dinner together, told stories, discussed our faith, got to know each other better, and laughed—a lot. The next day, I received a delightful email from the young woman thanking us for our hospitality and the love they had experienced in our home and among our family. She said that being in our home was "like a breath of fresh air" and that the love we radiate is "inspiring."

The young woman's email touched me deeply and I'm grateful, not only for her kind words, but for the opportunity to welcome these two wonderful individuals into our home. We were as much gifted and inspired by them as they were by us!

Later in the day, I spent some time meditating on her message. I don't consider our family extraordinary—I think all families are beautiful and inspiring in their own way. So I asked myself what it was that so affected our visitors. The answer was love.

Isn't that the mission of all families? Of all Christians? Are we not called to love after the example of our Lord?

On the Solemnity of the Most Holy Trinity, in 2006, Pope Benedict XVI spoke about the love of families to the crowd gathered in St. Peter's Square for the Angelus. He compared the family to the Holy Trinity, saying that it "is called to be a community of love and life, in which differences must come together to become a parable of communion."

He went on to say that, guided by the Holy Spirit, believers can know "the intimacy of God himself, discovering that he is not infinite solitude, but communion of light and love, life given and received in an eternal dialogue between the Father and the Son in the Holy Spirit—lover, beloved, and love."

So, too it is in the family—whether it's a biological family, a community of individuals, or the family of Holy Mother Church. We strive to know, love, and serve God in, with, and for one another. In our daily lives we enter into an eternal dialogue with the Father and Son in the Holy Spirit.

"And it is in this love," the Holy Father stated, "that the human being finds his truth and happiness."

That's our family mission. Our family *is* the mission. Not only do we share our love and devotion with the triune God, our Blessed Mother and each other, but also we share it with all who enter our home. No one is ever turned away from our door, and once inside, all are loved unconditionally regardless of who they are, what's been left behind, or what's transpired in the world outside of our walls. In our home, we constantly strive to reflect the Blessed Trinity by living an atmosphere of reverence, love, and readiness for sacrifice.

That doesn't mean we have a one-hundred-percent success rate. Believe me, we have our moments. But it's exactly those moments that make us realize how dependent we are on the triune God in our human frailty, how important our faith is, and how much we love and need each other after all. Experiencing those "moments" in our own family helps us to understand, accept, and forgive them in others. It's a continuous cycle of trying, falling, and getting up again—each time a bit stronger than the last.

The family mission looks different in each family. For some, it's more active and extroverted. For others, it's more contemplative and introverted. For others, it's a shifting combination of both. But for all families, it's a call to do our best to reflect the Holy Trinity in all that we think, do, and say. With the guidance and education of our Blessed Mother, and through the graces she distributes, may all who enter our homes find them to be a breath of fresh air and be inspired by the love that we radiate.

## What does Scripture say?

*For this reason I bow my knees before the Father, from whom every family in heaven and on earth takes its name. I pray that, according to the riches of his glory, he may grant that you may be strengthened in your inner being with power through his*

*Spirit, and that Christ may dwell in your hearts through faith, as you are being rooted and grounded in love. I pray that you may have the power to comprehend, with all the saints, what is the breadth and length and height and depth, and to know the love of Christ that surpasses knowledge, so that you may be filled with all the fullness of God.*

EPHESIANS 3:14–19

## What does my heart say?

∎ What does Saint Paul mean by "from whom every family in heaven and on earth is named"?
∎ What is the breadth and length and height and depth of Christian love?
∎ How would I describe the eternal dialogue between the Father, Son, and Holy Spirit?

∎ ∎ ∎ ∎

# Settling Our Differences

MARK AND I have created a trio of monsters. We've gone overboard in teaching our children to explore the world around them and be more independent and responsible.

At ages seven-and-a-half, four-and-a-half, and two, our children's management styles have already begun to emerge. However, what they've emerged into is complete atrophy.

This diversity shows itself most noticeably in the way they tackle projects like cleaning their bedrooms. Matthew, our oldest, manages by dissection and abandonment. Whatever the task at hand, he spends magnanimous amounts of time taking every possible component apart (even ones having nothing to do with the original project). He scatters the pieces far and wide, labeling this "sorting." Hours later, discouraged, confused, and just plain bored, he drops everything and moves on to something else.

Monica, whose four-and-a-half-year-old mind works on a level none of us can reach, follows this rule of thumb: be brief, be simple, and never pay attention to details. She does her work by flitting around, brushing everything into piles in discreet little corners. Then, she quickly wipes her hands and declares the task "all done."

And Luke? What can I say about a two-year-old who governs his world by literally throwing his weight around? Woe to anyone in his way.

Mark, very patient, constantly encourages the children to take their time so they can do it right the first time. I, on the other hand, am a human catalyst. I tell them, "Just hurry up and get it done. Then you'll have time to do something else."

Often, as I settle down to sleep at night, I think about the day gone by. What did we accomplish as a family? What were our failures? What did we do well? What could we have done better?

This usually leads me to the same conclusion: Wouldn't things go more smoothly if we were all alike? If only Monica had some of Matthew's detail-orientation. If only Matthew had some of Monica's casualness. If only I had more of Mark's patience, and he had more of my drive. If only Luke could teach us all his gift of momentum and motivation…

Then I start thinking about the heavenly Father. He knows all and sees all. If our tiny family finds it hard to work with our five personality differences, what must it be like to watch a whole world full of different people all trying to get along together? If it irritates me to see our family work in opposite directions, doesn't it bug him to see an earth full of people going in circles?

What's the key to getting this big, wide world to work together in harmony? Not assimilation; I've tried that in our family. It doesn't work.

Then amalgamation? That's more likely. It seems as though the better way is to take each of our styles, skills, ideas, and hopes and put them together towards our common goal—bringing the world to Christ. That means learning from one another and giving thanks to God for the beauty of our differences.

That isn't easy. We're called to a great task, and at times it's hard to believe that God chose *us* to do the job.

That must be the way my children feel when I ask them to do something. They probably can't believe I chose *them* to do the job. But, differences or not, we've been chosen. Here we are with the task before us. We can either let our differences deter us from our goal or strengthen us in our mission.

And my family? Well, considering the circumstances and the persons involved, I'd say the goal is survival.

## What does Scripture say?

> *For who sees anything different in you? What do you have that you did not receive? And if you received it, why do you boast as if it were not a gift?*
>
> 1 CORINTHIANS 4:7

## What does my heart say?

- **I** What do I like best about myself?
- **I** How do my friends and family describe me?
- **I** What is it that sets me apart from others?

❙  ❙  ❙  ❙

# Maybe I'm Crazy After All...

THE WORST PART was that I really liked her. From the moment I entered her office, I felt an immediate rapport with this young female doctor. She was bright, bubbly, and had a great sense of humor.

I had come to the northern Wisconsin clinic while on a family vacation because I was experiencing some signs of miscarriage and was seeking medical advice. The nurse assured me that this young woman was an excellent professional, and I believed her. The doctor and I seemed to understand each other and had a lot in common. She examined me and ordered some tests. Things were going very well until she said something that made me bristle.

"You know, Margaret, if the test results are beyond what we'd like to see, which I expect they may be, I strongly suggest that you consider terminating the pregnancy," she said matter-of-factly.

TERMINATE THE PREGNANCY! It was as if she expected me to throw away my child like a botched batch of cookies. I couldn't understand how someone who had spent all those years in medical school learning how to preserve life could even think of indiscriminately ending it. What's more, she said it with such ease. She didn't really believe abortion was a reasonable solution, did she? Completely shocked, all I managed to mutter was, "No." That was hardly the response I would have imagined myself giving had I known in advance what she was going to say.

The rest of the office visit was a blur; my vision colored by my disappointment in the viewpoint of this vivacious, progressive, and intelligent obstetrician. I looked at her wedding ring and wondered if she had ever considered terminating any of her own pregnancies. I looked at her long, flowing skirt and peasant blouse, which I had been admiring just moments ago. I liked the way she had broken away from the traditional stuffy doctors' garb. I looked at her gentle hands, which had welcomed so many little people into the world. I tried to gaze deep into her brilliant eyes to find some hint that she hadn't really meant what she said. But I found none. I was hurt, disheartened, and even a bit frightened. All I wanted to do was get out of that office—fast.

A while ago, I read an article quoting Mother Teresa of Calcutta as she addressed those in attendance at the National Prayer Breakfast on February 3, 1994, in Washington, D.C. She warned that violence against the unborn begets all forms of violence.

"If we accept that a mother can kill even her own child, how can we tell other people not to kill each other? …Any country that accepts abortion is not teaching its people to love, but to use violence to get what they want," she said.

When I think back to the young doctor's flippant attitude toward murdering my child, what Mother Teresa said rings ever more loudly in my ears. When mothers who are meant to nurture life are pressured to destroy it, we negate the most essential element of motherhood. Without true motherhood, there can be no true fatherhood. Nor can there be true childhood. Without those essential roles filled, a family-centered society dissolves into a heathen society.

The northern Wisconsin obstetrician isn't the only one who felt the same about my pregnancy. The doctor who performed the pregnancy test at my family clinic asked me four or five times if this pregnancy was "all right" with me. What was he expecting me to say? "No, doctor. It's obvious that God has made a mistake here. Let's just kill the baby and fix that mistake." The prenatal nurse assigned to my case was required by "normal" procedures to conduct an in-depth analysis of my marital relationship and the circumstances surrounding the conception of my child. She even offered me psychological counseling because "after all, it's the fourth pregnancy, and well…" Well what? I wasn't aware that being pregnant a fourth time made me a candidate for the mental institution!

Then again, maybe I am crazy after all. I'm crazy about the teachings of the Church. I'm crazy about the sanctity of life from conception until natural death. I'm crazy enough to see a pregnancy through, no matter how difficult it may be. I'm crazy about the blessings that pour forth every time a child of God is born.

## What does Scripture say?

*I call heaven and earth to witness against you today that I have set before you life and death, blessings and curses. Choose life so that you and your descendants may live, loving the LORD your God, obeying him, and holding fast to him; for that means life to you and length of days, so that you may live in the land that the LORD swore to give to your ancestors, to Abraham, to Isaac, and to Jacob.*

DEUTERONOMY 30:19–20

## What does my heart say?

‖ Was there a time in my life when someone thought I was crazy because of my beliefs?

‖ Why did he or she react that way?

‖ How did I react?

■ ▮ ▮ ■
# Used Books

I WAS SO NERVOUS when I walked down the hall that my knees wobbled as I took each step; my teeth felt chattery, like those rattling dentures you see in the cartoons. In spite of my nerves, I tried to look as confident and young as possible—anything to hide the fact that it'd been more than twenty years since I'd been a college student.

It was two weeks before classes began, and I wanted to mosey about, get a feel for the campus, and pick up the textbook for the course I was taking. I hoped to get the "feel" of being a twenty-first-century student so that I wouldn't make a spectacle of myself before I even entered the classroom on the first day.

Following the signs and stopping now and then for directions, I wound my way around the hallways until I finally found the university bookstore. I glanced through the window to count heads, get the basic layout, and spot potentials for embarrassment. Then I took a deep breath and went in. I was greeted by a smartly-dressed woman, just a bit older than me.

"Can I help you?" she asked sweetly.

"Uh, yes," I stammered, trying not to sound like a confused forty-something-year-old. "I'm looking for the text for Counseling 593."

"Rob," she said to the *very* young man behind the counter, "could you please help this young lady find what she needs?"

I loved that wise, perceptive woman from the second she opened her mouth.

"Sure," Rob said casually as he swung his long, dangly bangs to the other side of his forehead and stepped out from behind the counter. "Over here."

*How'd this kid get into college?* I wondered to myself. He looked like he should be selling lemonade on the street corner. He led me to the back of the store and down a narrow aisle.

"Right there," he said, pointing to a section of books on the lower shelf. He must have sensed my uncertainty, because he leaned over, picked up a textbook and handed it to me.

"Here. This is what you're looking for," he reassured me.

"Is it just this one book that I need for the course?" I asked.

"Yeah," he replied knowingly.

I fingered the book while Rob looked over my shoulder. It didn't look too far above sea level—I should be able to wade through it. I was even starting to get excited about being a student again.

"Uh, where's the price?" I asked.

"Right there," he said, pointing to a sign below the pile of books. I asked him to confirm which number he was pointing to.

After he pointed it out a second time, I exclaimed, "That? That's the price? Oh, my goodness! I thought that was the ID number!"

Rob's eyebrows shot up and he just stood there, staring at me.

I swallowed hard and tried to get hold of my wits so I wouldn't seem as stupid as I felt. I looked at the price again and sighed. I really was looking forward to getting a brand new book, but the price was pretty high. Resignedly, I asked Rob where the used books were. His eyebrows shot up again.

"Those *are* the used books," he replied incredulously.

There was no getting around that one. I'd made a fool of myself and now the only option was to get out of there as gracefully—and quickly—as possible.

I thanked Rob for his help, awkwardly paid for my textbook, and left.

On the drive home, I thought about the ridiculousness of the situation. There I was, wishing to slip into the college scene unnoticed, and instead I ended up drawing attention to myself. I wanted a brand new book, and instead our Lord told me that a used one would be good enough. I wanted to seem "with it," and instead God gave me a whopping dose of humility.

I laughed quietly as I sped down the highway toward home. That word "instead" is a powerful one. I've had plenty of "insteads" in my life. Countless times, I've aimed at one goal only to find that our Lord wanted me to aim for another one instead. I constantly petition him for the things I think I need, but he gives me something else instead. I want to be treated delicately, and instead he ruffles my feathers and hurls me into a wind tunnel. It's always "used books" instead of "new ones."

Usually I fight with all my willpower to avoid the used books— at least initially. But when I discover that the new books cost far too much, I sigh resignedly and wander back to the used bookshelf, because those are the ones that are best for me.

## What does Scripture say?

> *But there are also many other things that Jesus did; if every one of them were written down, I suppose that the world itself could not contain the books that would be written.*

JOHN 21:25

## What does my heart say?

- **I** What are the "used books" in my life?
- **I** When was the last time I was given a "new book" that I didn't like?
- **I** When was the last time I was given a "used book" that turned out to be better than the "new book" I'd anticipated?

■ I I ■
# Thread of Life

MATTHEW LOOKED so handsome standing there in my father's old navy hat and leggings, with Dad's military green knapsack thrown across his shoulders. The sack was almost bigger than his eight-year-old body, but he didn't care. He stood there with pride, as straight as he could. My eyes teared and a huge lump filled my throat. I wanted to take him in my arms and hold him forever.

The children and I had been digging through an old trunk of family artifacts: Dad's navy souvenirs, Grandma's Sunday-best dickie, and Grandpa's cane and spats, among other treasures. Monica, five, and Luke, three, were having a great time with their big brother pretending about the "old days." I was having a great time watching their eyes light up as I told them stories about our family history.

I told them about the small farming village in Germany where my distant relatives had raised their families and my great-grandfather had been the mayor or "burgermeister." I told them about the serious old man I had lovingly nicknamed "Grumpa," who had immigrated to Milwaukee in 1924. After having found secure work and a decent place to live, he brought his new bride, Antonia, to Wisconsin. In 1927, she gave birth to their first child—my father, George.

Grandpa was a stouthearted and devout Catholic, but he was quiet about his faith. I'm sure he loved the Church, but he didn't seem to have the same sense of church community with which I was familiar. I wonder now if he had difficulty acclimating to changes in the liturgy after the Second Vatican Council. Hadn't he had enough to assimilate with a new country, a new culture, a new language and a new way of life?

He especially found the sign of peace during holy Mass distasteful; I think it was a real trial for him. Right after the Our Father, he would stick his hands down by his sides and look straight ahead, avoiding eye contact with the people around him. Once the sign of peace was over, he'd loosen up.

As a child, I was puzzled by Grandpa's response to what I saw as a normal part of the Mass. It seemed strange to decline the opportunity to reach out to those around you, especially when you were in a church filled with people within easy reach. I knew Grandpa was a serious person, but I never thought of him as cold.

Growing up, I was better able to understand Grandpa's ways. I think that for him, faith was a private affair. Church was a place to connect directly with our Lord, rather than a place to connect with our fellow man. Perhaps he saw the sign of peace as a mere form of socialization extraneous to the real meaning of the Mass.

I smiled to myself as I recalled that Matt was a fairly serious person and didn't care much for the sign of peace, either. Of course, Matt's reasons were of shyness and not theology, but I was struck by the traits that he shared with my grandfather, a man whom he had never met.

Matt inherited more than personality traits from Grandpa. He, along with our other children, inherited the riches of our Catholic faith. The kids are even more blessed to have inherited the faith through not one, but two family trees—my husband's and mine. For as many generations back as we can trace, the Catholic faith has wound it's way through our families like a thread of life binding us all to one another.

The same thread winds its way through all Catholic families. Even if the faith can't be traced for generations back in our genealogy, it can be traced back through the centuries of the holy Catholic Church—Christ's family. All who belong to the Church are members of his Mystical Body. We're bound together by the thread of eternal life.

Wouldn't it be great if from time to time we could dig through the old trunk of family artifacts and cherish the memories of the "old days"? Perhaps there's a child inside each of us waiting to don the old navy cap, leggings, and knapsack. It's possible, and we can do it anytime we wish. There are volumes of artifacts and memories available to us, from Scripture to the stories of the saints to the writings of the popes. There's a plentitude of pilgrimage places and parish churches that hold within their walls the histories of Catholics who have come and gone long ago. The trunk is there, waiting for us to open it and discover the thread of life that binds us all together.

## What does Scripture say?

*Now to him who by the power at work within us is able to accomplish abundantly far more than all we can ask or imagine, to him be glory in the church and in Christ Jesus to all generations, for ever and ever. Amen.*

EPHESIANS 3:20–21

## What does my heart say?

❙ What kind of faith have I inherited through my family?
❙ What do I consider to be my place in the Catholic Church?
❙ Of the traditions I've inherited through my Catholic faith, what do I most treasure?

▌ ▌ ▌ ▌

# Master Game Maker

JOHN GOT a Mouse Trap Game for his sixth birthday. If you've never played it, you're really missing something. Mouse Trap is an intriguing array of rickety old stairs, suspended bathtubs, winding chutes, wheels, cranks, and even a catapulting skydiver. Players build the spectacle as they progress around the game board, winning pieces of cheese as they go along. The object is to trap the other players' mice in a little cage that comes plummeting down on top of them. The last "free" rodent wins.

Generally, John's a very loving and generous kid. But whenever anyone else wins Mouse Trap, he's scandalized. You might think it's due to an out-of-whack competitive nature, but it's not. John likes to come out on top like most of us, but it's not in him to crush others just to get ahead. He's not afraid to lose, either, although he's not overjoyed by it. No, the problem with someone else winning Mouse Trap is that it's HIS game. Therefore, he feels that *he* should be the one to win it. Every time.

I've tried repeatedly to motherly and affectionately reason with him, but to no avail. I've tried to explain to John that the winner of the game is not determined by who owns it, but he'll have none of that. Telling him that it's up to chance would be even worse because, thanks to our incessant drilling, he believes that everything that happens is part of God's loving plan for us. And what kind of god would make a kid lose his own Mouse Trap Game?

"John, I can see you're upset that you didn't win the game," I say to his sweaty, tear-washed head that is buried in my lap. "But you can't expect to win every game. Sometimes you'll win, and sometimes someone else will win."

He says nothing, as smothered siren cries rise from my rapidly soaking lap.

"John? Did you hear what I said? Do you understand that we all take turns being winners and losers?" I prod.

John heaves a huge sigh, "Yes, I KNOW that. I KNOW I have to lose sometimes…but not MY game!"

Then it's my turn to sigh as I tenderly stroke his bewildered head. How very childish he is. He still has much to learn about life, and it's difficult to teach him how to be accepting when things don't turn out his way. He can't understand that the pieces aren't always going to go together the way he expects them to. No matter how I try, he just doesn't see it.

He sounds just like…me. I can be very childish at times—I hate to lose my own game! I hate it when the wheels and cranks don't turn in the way I want. I absolutely abhor it when someone else gets to take a piece of cheese and not me. I hate to give up a turn, lose a chance to erect part of the trap, or do something that I don't want to do. No one can tell me to calm down when something happens that I deem unfair. Worst of all, I can't stand it when I'm planning on one course of action and the mousetrap comes plummeting down on top of me.

The game I'm talking about here, of course, isn't some inconsequential board game. I'm referring to life itself. Isn't it just like a game? We're always moving forwards and backwards, always at the mercy of someone else's moves, always facing the unexpected. And just when we think we've decided on a course of action, we suddenly find ourselves landing on the "Go Back to Start" space. This is my game—my life—and I want to be the one to say when and how I'm going to move. I want to be the winner of my own game.

If I weren't so childish, I'd realize that the game I play isn't mine at all. The Master Game Maker created it for me. Yes, it's a gift, but it isn't really mine to keep. I'm only the player at the mercy of the rules and chances, twists and turns, worked into the game by its creator. I have some choices—I can decide if I want to take the cheese or set up the rickety stairs, for instance—but it's up to him whether I'm caught in the trap at the end. It's all a matter of a roll of the dice.

It's a relief to know that the power behind the dice is a benevolent one! My Master Game Maker assures that every roll lands in the way that's best for me. It may not seem like the opportune moment, but he knows exactly when to catapult my skydiver. When I've made the wrong choice, he mercifully and gently puts me on the "Go Back to Start" space. From my perspective, the game at times may seem perplexing and aggravating. I may rant and rave because my bathtub has collapsed. I may become completely confused because I can't move and wonder where all my cheese has gone. But it's my own near-sightedness and ignorance that keeps me from being able to see the way the board is laid out before me. If I could do that, I would certainly find much more pleasure and relaxation in playing the game.

Instead I bury my head in my Blessed Mother's lap, cry smothered siren cries, and complain that I KNOW I have to lose sometimes… but not MY game! Then it's her turn to sigh as she tenderly strokes my bewildered head.

## What does Scripture say?

> *When I was a child, I spoke like a child, I thought like a child, I reasoned like a child; when I became an adult, I put an end to childish ways. For now we see in a mirror, dimly, but then we will see face to face. Now I know only in part; then I will know fully, even as I have been fully known. And now faith, hope, and love abide, these three; and the greatest of these is love.*

> 1 CORINTHIANS 13:11–13

## What does my heart say?

I In what ways am I childish?
I In what areas of my life do I most hate to lose? Why?

# ■ ■ ■ ■
# Turkey Hunt

THERE WE WERE, she on her side of the freezer case of the supermarket and I on mine, feverishly digging through frozen turkeys. We had switched sides a number of times, and by now had reorganized the entire one-hundred-fifty piece gobbler collection.

Suddenly, we stopped and looked up at each other.

"I bet I know what you're looking for," I said with a smirk.

"And I bet I know what *you're* looking for," the pleasant, middle-aged woman smirked back.

In unison, we threw up our hands and called out, "A fifteen-pound turkey!"

Sure enough. There were ten-pounders, eleven-pounders, and twenty-something-pounders, but nothing in-between.

"Okay," I said playfully. "Let's both dig, and whoever comes up with a fifteen-pounder first, wins! Ready? Go!"

She laughed, and we continued our search. After some time of fruitless shuffling, I began to lose hope. In the meantime, another woman had joined our turkey hunt.

Finally, I gave in. Thinking of the number of mouths we have to feed at home, I resigned myself to a bigger bird. "Darn. I guess I'll just take one of the twenty-pounders," I told the first woman. "I've still got four at home."

The second woman turned to me, wide-eyed, and exclaimed, "You've got four turkeys at home!?"

With a wink and a wry smile, I looked at her and said, "Well, sometimes they are."

I chuckled at the quizzical look on her face. She, of course, was thinking about Thanksgiving turkeys, and I was thinking about turkeys of a different kind—my four children.

They aren't really turkeys, but they sometimes act like it when they demonstrate their wild sense of humor (now, where do they get *that* from?) or exercise their mischievous side. They can be hard to handle at times, and they can be quite elusive at others—just like a fifteen-pound turkey in a supermarket freezer case.

Regardless, I wouldn't want to be without them for a second, and I'd search every freezer case in the world a hundred times over just to have them. Every bit of the difficulty bringing them into this world has been worth it—the fretful, high-risk pregnancies; critical births; the countless hours standing beside isolettes and gazing at infants barely clinging to life; the tubes, wires, and monitors; the anguished waiting for weeks to hold them for the first time. I would do it all again.

Then there are the ups and downs of raising them: the laughter and goofing around; tears, arguments and misunderstandings; funky music; family movie nights and summer vacations; bowls upon bowls of popcorn; long, private talks and the silent treatment; crises and pleasant surprises; letting go when I wanted to pull them closer; pushing away when they clung too tightly; all the joys and sorrows big and small—they have all been worth the privilege of parenting these incredible human beings.

Over the years, we've come to be known as the Fenelon Clan. Part of the reason is that we wanted to distinguish ourselves from the rest of Mark's rather large extended family. The main reason is because that's just who we are. We're the Fenelon Clan. We've survived some fairly hair-raising experiences and have managed, through God's grace and mercy, to come out on top. We're not perfect, but we're certainly stronger, wiser, and more unified because of it.

Before long, the kids will be going off to find their own lives and vocations. Perhaps they'll become clergy or religious; perhaps they'll go off to start their own clans. No matter where they go or what they do, they'll take with them the guts and gumption to see it through and the dependence on God's grace and mercy that they've learned from being a part of the Fenelon Clan.

Maybe then I'll be hunting through the freezer case for a different-size turkey. For now, I've still got four at home.

## What does Scripture say?

*You will be enriched in every way for your great generosity, which will produce thanksgiving to God through us; for the rendering of this ministry not only supplies the needs of the saints but also overflows with many thanksgivings to God.*

2 CORINTHIANS 9:11–12

## What does my heart say?

▌ What are some of the hard-earned joys and privileges God has led me to in my life?

▌ What did he ask of me along the way?

▌ How am I stronger from those experiences?

# FEAST DAYS

## MARY, MOTHER OF GOD
### Goodbye to You.
### Goodbye to You-ou-ou...

A SONG with those lines in it has been rambling around in my head for days. I think it's because yesterday was Monica's nineteenth birthday, and it occurred to me that this is her last year as a teenager. In three hundred sixty-four short days, she'll experience the right of passage that moves the first digit of the age counter clicker from one to two. The years of hanging out and going with the flow will shift into the world of adult responsibilities.

This means my curly-headed little blondie is becoming a self-sufficient woman. It's not that I don't want her to grow up...I just wish she'd slow down a bit. She's our only daughter—the only other female in the house besides me (and the dog, but she doesn't count). She's the only other one who understands I'm having "one of those days" just because I'm having one of those days. She's the only one who can spot the sparkly red elevator shoes in the bottom of the thrift shop bin. There's no one else here who understands that when I need chocolate, I NEED chocolate.

Thank God Monica will be around for a while yet, but her birthday was a stark reminder that things won't be this way forever. Eventually all the kids will grow up and leave the nest. Then Mark and I will have to find other ways to occupy ourselves. I'm sure things will pop up that will naturally fill in the gaps, but life will be different, and I'm not a fan of different. Especially *that* kind of different.

I wonder if the Mother of our Lord ever felt like that. Think of all the changes—all the "differents" that she faced in her life. She gave birth to the long-awaited Messiah, and then had to scurry off to Egypt to protect his life. She had to get used to a new culture, a new language, and a new way of life. Then, she's back at Nazareth, getting used to the *old* different. What about finding Jesus in the Temple? She lost one son only to find a different one, one who had grown in wisdom and stature and must now be about his Father's business. A little respite followed, and things in Nazareth seemed fairly sane. That is until she lost her husband. There wasn't a whole lot of breathing space before her son began his public ministry. Things were certainly different at that point. Now her son was a prophet, a miracle worker, and a hunted man. The trial before Pilate, the crucifixion, resurrection, and ascension were all huge "differents." How different was it to be in the midst of the early church? Finally, she was assumed into heaven and was given the eternal different.

I often wonder if she had any idea what it would be like when she said "yes" to becoming the Mother of God. I imagine she expected the usual. Children grow and become less dependent on their parents. They enter adulthood and leave the home. They form their own lives. But could she have had any clue of both the magnificence and horror she'd witness in the future?

One of my favorite Scripture passages about the Blessed Mother is from Saint Luke's Gospel. She'd just given birth to the Savior—in a cave filled with animals, nonetheless. Shepherds were showing up with some cockamamie story about angels appearing to them because of her baby, and royal astrologers from goodness-knows-where approached, claiming to have been signaled by some kind of majestic star. What's her response?

"But Mary treasured all these words and pondered them in her heart" (2:19).

Imagine that. All of these things were swirling about her and she wasn't shaken for a minute. She accepted it all calmly, trusting in God to help her go with the flow. Not only that, but she pondered them; she kept them in her heart and contemplated the message behind each event, each "different." What a model of the confident child Mary is!

I should meditate more on Mary's response to the "differents" in her life so that I can learn to respond more confidently to the differents in my own life. She was—is—the Mother of God, and yet she meets this tremendous honor and responsibility by pondering it in her heart.

It looks like I have some pondering of my own to do. Goodbye to you. Goodbye to you-ou-ou...

## What does Scripture say?

*So they went with haste and found Mary and Joseph, and the child lying in the manger. When they saw this, they made known what had been told them about this child; and all who heard it were amazed at what the shepherds told them. But Mary treasured all these words and pondered them in her heart.*

LUKE 2:16–19

## What does my heart say?

**I** What are the "differents" in my life?
**I** How have I handled them?
**I** What does pondering look like for me?

❚ ❙ ❙ ❚

# DIVINE MERCY SUNDAY
## Try Praying—For Somebody Else

FOR THE FIRST TIME in fifteen years of freelance writing, I was about to fail. I'd taken on an extremely important assignment on an extremely tight deadline and now I was about to pay for my folly. It was the story of a pregnant woman whose brain ceased to function and the family's courageous fight to save the child's life. They desperately needed help raising funds to pay the astronomical medical costs of keeping the woman's body on life support until the pregnancy progressed far enough along for the baby to be viable. Additionally, they would incur the expense of neonatal intensive care for a premature infant. Giving their situation media attention would help generate the prayer and financial support they needed. How could I *not* agree to help this family by writing an article about them?

It was the eleventh hour, and my editor was anxiously waiting for me to come in with this story. He'd slated it for the front page. Without my story to fill the space, things could get messy for him, and I didn't want that to happen. I also didn't want to miss the opportunity to tell the world about such an extraordinary family.

For the past three days, I'd been begging, pleading, sacrificing—everything short of jumping through burning hoops—to convince God to grant me the key interview I needed to finish the story. Now I was at the absolute final moment. I knew that, by the end of the day, my byline would read either "correspondent" or "mud."

As it neared three o'clock, I began to sweat. All I could think of was my impending deadline and my reputation as a writer. I rubbed my damp palms on my pant legs and prepared to say the Chaplet of Divine Mercy. I was about to offer it in petition for the interview I was seeking, but suddenly changed my mind. I was just plain tired of praying for this interview and decided to offer the chaplet for somebody else instead. Just as I started warming up the beads, the clock hit three and the phone rang. It was the person I'd been waiting to interview. By three-thirty, I had sent in the assignment, complete with the missing interview.

As I pushed the send button, I chuckled to myself. It seemed as if God was just waiting for me to turn my attention to someone else before he agreed to grant my petition. Certainly there is no harm in praying for ourselves—he answers those prayers in the way that's best for us. But there's something about the prayers said for others that must please the heavenly Father in a special way. Imagine the joy of a human father when one of his children does something for the sake of a brother or sister. We're doing the same thing when we pray for others, as we are all offspring of the same heavenly Father.

Is that why he urged me to say the Divine Mercy Chaplet for one of my brothers and sisters in Christ? Perhaps he wanted to remind me of the overflowing nature of his mercy. Perhaps he wanted me to see that when we show others mercy, they show mercy to yet others. In the interim, we draw mercy down upon ourselves. Once we begin the outward flow of mercy, we never know where it will flow next or where it will end up.

Our Lord told Blessed Faustina, "…I want to pour out my divine life into human souls and sanctify them, if only they were willing to accept my grace. The greatest sinners would achieve great sanctity, if only they would trust in my mercy. The very inner depths of my being are filled to overflowing with mercy, and it is being poured out upon all I have created. My delight is to act in a human soul and to fill it with my mercy and to justify it. My kingdom on earth is my life in the human soul" (*Divine Mercy in My Soul,* Marian Press, 1987).

We bring about that kingdom on earth when we pray for one another and thus share in God's infinite mercy. I wonder if we can adequately envision the good that is affected when we put the needs of another before our own. For many years, I've had the custom of offering a brief spontaneous prayer for persons who come into my mind from time to time during the day. I have no idea what effect my prayers have had on these people, and I probably never will. Nor will I have any idea of the effect my chaplet has had on the persons for whom I offered it the day of my deadline. I do know one thing, however. Next time, if all else fails, I'll try praying for somebody else.

## What does Scripture say?

*"Blessed are the merciful, for they will receive mercy."*

MATTHEW 5:7

## What does my heart say?

- **I** When have I shown mercy to another person?
- **I** When have I experienced God's mercy?
- **I** What are the differences and similarities between the two situations?

**I I I I**

# PENTECOST
## Divine Masterpieces

I LOVE taking ten-year-old John to swim class. It's one of the highlights of my week. It's certainly not the water I'm attracted to; I don't know how to swim. I don't even like being wet. No, I like to take him because the lessons are held in an intergenerational day care facility—one of those wonderful places in which people of all ages and stages of ability or disability are compassionately tended.

Every Wednesday afternoon, we pull into the parking lot and tuck the van into a slot. Then John grabs his swim gear and we head for the front entrance, which usually has a transport van or two idling in the half circle drive. We scoot past the exhaust fumes and wiggle our way around the attendants standing outside.

Just inside the electronic front door is one of the most beautiful sights an eye can behold: a menagerie of wheel chairs and walkers filled with some of the most joyful, innocent faces I've ever seen. They belong to mentally disabled people.

I especially like to look into their pure, loving, and unpretentious eyes. In them, I can see the face of God. They're not like those of us with more sophisticated thinking patterns. We fall prey to the mass-mindedness of society and devastation of the culture of death. We contrive and rationalize until even the most horrible deed can seem benevolent. Their hearts and minds are simple and untainted—they can only give and accept love. They're divine masterpieces.

If our hearts were as uncomplicated as theirs, we would never let our insecurities govern our actions and attitudes. We would never rationalize our disobedience to God's will. We would never be deceitful, conniving, or judgmental of others. We wouldn't crave power or seek revenge. Instead, we'd live our lives in complete acceptance and simplicity, content to be who we are and to trustingly follow God's plan for us.

When we open ourselves to the Holy Spirit, we also become divine masterpieces. With his seven gifts—wisdom, understanding, counsel, fortitude, knowledge, piety, fear of the Lord; and twelve fruits—charity, joy, peace, patience, kindness, goodness, generosity, gentleness, faithfulness, modesty, self-control, and chastity—he transforms our hearts and minds. Through his inspiration, we can put aside our sophisticated thinking patterns and reject the allures and ambitions that can abound not only in the culture around us, but in our own communities, workplaces, homes, and hearts.

The Blessed Virgin Mary is our best example; She's the vessel of the Holy Spirit. In the creed we say that she "conceived by the power of the Holy Spirit." She was so open to the Spirit's gifts and fruits, so pure in her longing for God, so eager to follow God's will, that his Son was formed in her womb!

Perhaps we can receive the Holy Spirit's gifts and fruits anew at Pentecost. Although we can't conceive of the Holy Spirit and bear the Son of God as the Blessed Mother did, we *can* conceive from the Holy Spirit a new attitude and zeal for God. If we mentally and spiritually seclude ourselves in the Upper Room with our Blessed Mother and the apostles, the Spirit will come and fill us with his presence.

"When the day of Pentecost had come, they were all together in one place. And suddenly from heaven there came a sound like the rush of a violent wind, and it filled the entire house where they were sitting. Divided tongues, as of fire, appeared among them, and a tongue rested on each of them. All of them were filled with the Holy Spirit and began to speak in other languages as the Spirit gave them ability" (Acts 2:1–4).

Those beautiful faces at the care facility remind me of the apostles in the Upper Room at Pentecost. As the wind blew and the tongues of fire appeared, they must have been so filled with love and joy that only the present moment mattered. That's just how many mentally disabled people approach life. Nothing else matters to them but the wonder and awe of the present moment.

The wind may not blow and tongues of fire may not appear for us this Pentecost. But the Spirit will come if we're open to him. If we allow him to, he'll transform us so that, when others look into our eyes, they'll see the face of God.

## What does Scripture say?

*Likewise the Spirit helps us in our weakness; for we do not know how to pray as we ought, but that very Spirit intercedes with sighs too deep for words. And God, who searches the heart, knows what is the mind of the Spirit, because the Spirit intercedes for the saints according to the will of God.*

ROMANS 8:26–27

## What does my heart say?

▮ What is my relationship with the Holy Spirit?
▮ How would I describe the "sighs too deep for words"?
▮ What prompts them?

∎ ∎ ∎ ∎

# ASCENSION
## Lost and Found

THERE WAS an article in this morning's newspaper about a fifty-six-year-old man who's been missing for more than three months. His body was found two nights ago in Lake Michigan, near our home. The fact that the man, a loving husband and respected bank executive, was from the town right next to ours had a strange impact on me.

When the story first broke about his disappearance, it gave me an eerie feeling, mostly because it's so close to home (physically), but also because...because...I don't know why. I think it might be overflow from Matt's deployment in the Middle East with the Wisconsin National Guard. Your loved one isn't around, and you're not positively sure he's ever coming back.

I thought often about this man and prayed for him and for his family every time I ran across one of those missing-person flyers scattered around town. They were everywhere—the post office, grocery store, bank, bike shop, and plastered on telephone poles up and down the streets. I couldn't imagine how awful it would be to have a loved one suddenly gone without a trace.

The circumstances of the discovery of the man's body are amazing. His thirteen-year-old niece prayed at the lakeshore to Saint Anthony for help finding her uncle. Fifteen minutes later, the body was found very close to where the prayer had been uttered. Good ol' Saint Anthony. No one knows how the man's body ended up in Lake Michigan, nor do they know the cause for his disappearance. All they knew was that what had been lost was found.

The news article described the family's relief at having found their missing member and their conviction that he's now in a better place— with his Father in heaven. I was touched by their strength, their faith, and their inspiring hope of seeing him again in eternity.

This account made me think of the apostles after the crucifixion.

Their loved one, a victim of unfortunate circumstances, was gone, and they weren't positively sure he was ever coming back. Then came the resurrection, with its miraculous reunion! What a glorious time that must have been for them as they again gathered, shared meals, laughed, sang, talked, and learned from their revered teacher and rabbi. What had been lost was found. Forty days later, their Lord left them again, ascending into heaven in a brilliant blur. What sorrow and confusion they must have felt. Their loved one was no longer around, and they weren't positively sure he was ever coming back.

He left behind something very important, however. He left behind the promise that he would send the Paraclete, the Consoler who would encourage, sustain and guide them in his absence. He would send the Holy Spirit with his fruits and gifts to help them carry on the mission he'd given to them. Not only that, but he also left himself: body, blood, soul, and divinity in the holy Eucharist. They had much more than just memories to sustain them in Jesus' absence.

So too, for us. We might sometimes feel as though our loved one is gone and we're not positively sure if he's ever coming back. Perhaps it's not a person we've lost, but a part of ourselves. Perhaps we've watched hopes and dreams float away in a blur, never to return. Perhaps something we put our blood, sweat, and tears into was swept out from under us. Or maybe we feel a loss that we can't define.

The Ascension isn't the end of the story; it's the beginning. Jesus now sits at the right hand of his Father. We meet him again in every human being we encounter. We unite with him in every holy Eucharist. We experience him in the presence of the Holy Spirit. It might at times feel as though our loved One is gone and we're not positively sure he's ever coming back, but that's not the case. He's here. He's right among us, around us, within us. He's not gone, and we *can* be positively sure that he's coming back.

## What does Scripture say?

*"But I have said these things to you so that when their hour comes
you may remember that I told you about them.*

*"I did not say these things to you from the beginning, because
I was with you. But now I am going to him who sent me; yet none
of you asks me, 'Where are you going?' But because I have said
these things to you, sorrow has filled your hearts. Nevertheless
I tell you the truth: it is to your advantage that I go away, for if
I do not go away, the Advocate will not come to you; but if I go,
I will send him to you."*

JOHN 16:4–7

## What does my heart say?

I What are one or two of the lost and found moments I've
experienced in my life?

I What was the "lost" moment like?

I What was the "found" moment like?

▮ ▮ ▮ ▮

# ASSUMPTION
## Wilted Roses

THE POOR THING'S head was hanging so far down that the stem was nearly bent. The petals had a kind of sorry, sideways lean that made them look like the unhinged jaws of a snake, dismally hoping for prey to cross its path. Surely it was doomed.

The other rose wasn't quite as bad. Its head was dipping, but the stem seemed strong and the petals were still neatly spiraled. It looked like it had a fairly good chance of surviving and reaching full bloom.

The roses were a special gift from the kids to Mark, and we had wanted to enjoy them for as long as possible. I carefully arranged them in a vase, tenderly weaving them in among a bunch of miniature daisies, and propping their heads against the stems of the stronger flowers.

I placed the vase on the altar in our prayer corner and sighed, "Sorry, Blessed Mother. I wanted to share them with you, but I guess I left them out of water too long and killed them."

I stepped back and examined my handiwork. Then I folded my arms and shook my head. "Mark? Do you think I should just toss them out? Especially that one; I doubt it'll spring back to life."

"Yeah, I would," he responded. "At least they were nice while they lasted."

I reached for the vase and then withdrew my hand. I just couldn't bring myself to throw the roses away—at least not yet, anyway. It was late in the evening, and I decided that I'd leave them until morning to see what would happen.

"Well, Mother, it's up to you," I lamented as I went up to bed.

The next morning was such a flurry of activity that I almost forgot about the roses. We'd just gotten back from a family retreat, and there was a ton of unpacking and reorganizing to do. I grabbed a maverick prayer card and headed for the prayer corner. As I laid the card on the altar, I noticed the roses.

The one I had assumed was finished had not only survived and revived, but it had flourished to the point of being even more vivacious than the other! It was truly beautiful. I stood there for a while, admiring it and thinking about its close call with the trashcan the night before. I had been ready to do away with it simply because it appeared to be hopelessly wilted.

Isn't that the way it is with so many of the people and situations in our lives? Aren't they also like a wilted rose?

When someone in whom we placed our hope and trust doesn't live up to our expectations, we assume there's no possibility of change. When a relationship becomes strained and difficult, we assume there's no chance of revival. When a situation is so complicated that we can't seem to keep our heads up, we assume it's time to trash the whole thing. Perhaps sometimes we're the wilted ones and are tempted to give up on ourselves, because the stem seems far too bent.

That's the point at which we need to turn to our Mother and Queen in trustful surrender. Upon her glorious assumption, she was given intercessory powers that far exceed our limited human fathom ability. The Church calls her "Advocate, Helper, Benefactress, and Mediatrix" (*Catechism of the Catholic Church*, 969); these are the roles that she assumed when she entered eternity. In that respect, perhaps we could imagine that the word "assumption" means more than having both her unstained body and soul taken up into heaven. Her heart is open wide to her children; she's merely waiting for us to ask for the graces that she's privileged to mediate.

When we commit into her care the persons, relationships, and situations in our lives that seem doomed, she nurtures and restores them. When we commit into her care our needy and weak selves, she infuses us with grace and helps us to lift our heads again so we can continue blooming. If we entrust all to her, she assures us abundant fruitfulness even for the most wilted rose.

## What does Scripture say?

*I will be like the dew to Israel;*
*he shall blossom like the lily,*
*he shall strike root like the forests of Lebanon.*

HOSEA 14:5

## What does my heart say?

▌ Is there a wilted rose in my life that I've slated for the trash can?
▌ What would it take to revive it?
▌ How would I go about surrendering it to the care of the Blessed Mother?

■ ▌ ▌ ■

# ALL SAINTS
## Reality Check

THE OTHER DAY, we attended a family gathering at my brother-in-law's house. Relatives were in from out-of-state and it was one of the only opportunities for us all to be together at once while everyone was in town. In a family of twelve siblings and nearly as many in-laws, that's quite a feat! Mark and I had a previous engagement that day, so we sent the kids on ahead of us and arrived a bit later in the day.

I was completely shocked when I entered the house. It was like walking from stifling heat into frigid air conditioning. Actually, that's exactly what *did* happen. We were having some fantastic ninety-seven-degree weather. Ninety-seven might not be so bad to most folks, but when you add a thick layer of Wisconsin cut-through-it-with-a-knife humidity, whew! It's awful.

Temperatures aside, the real shock was looking around at all these people who are supposed to still be kids, but who have morphed into adults seemingly overnight. Good grief! They were everywhere—

nieces and nephews in adult form. Piggy-tails had turned into flirty flips, and pudgy kissy-cheeks had turned into scruffy goatees. Even worse, they had significant others with them—a double whammy. I felt overwhelmed and outnumbered. How could they do this to me?

Even my favorite godson had joined the pack. Of course, he's my *only* godson, which makes him an easy favorite.

The goofy part was seeing my own kids mixed into the lot. It was simply disgusting. You couldn't tell the nieces and nephews from the aunts and uncles. Well, with the exception of a salt 'n pepper head of hair here or there.

My shock became most apparent when I greeted my nephew's new wife. With a great big hug, I welcomed her into the family. "Hey, this makes you my sister-in-law now!" Her response was a blank look, which I couldn't figure out until I realized what I had just said. Trying to correct myself didn't do much good—I'd already shown my brilliance. *Sigh.*

With All Saints Day approaching, I've been thinking more and more about that family reunion. I see some of the relatives fairly often, some less often, and others rarely. Having them all together—both the familiar and less familiar—and seeing them interacting, reacquaint-ing, and reuniting gave me a small taste of what it might be like when we're all reunited in eternity.

I wonder what it'll be like to see the saints we've read about time and again. I have a personal checklist of folks I want to find when I enter the pearly gates. First, of course, I want to see our Lord and his Blessed Mother. After that, I want to see my dad, father-in-law, and then Father Joseph Kentenich. Then I want to assemble the apostles and hear each of their stories. I want to meet Mary Magdalene, Mar-garet Queen of Scots, Saint Francis de Sales, and Edith Stein. Oh, and I can't forget Saint Paul! There are so many saints with whom I'd like to converse that it's impossible to name them all.

I can't wait to experience that aspect of the communion of saints, which is the Church's term for all souls present on earth: those who have died and are being purified, and those who are in glory. The *Catechism of the Catholic Church* teaches us that "It is not merely by the title of example that we cherish the memory of those in heaven; we seek, rather, that by this devotion to the exercise of the fraternal charity the union of the whole Church in the Spirit may be strengthened. Exactly as Christian communion among our fellow pilgrims brings us closer to Christ, so our communion with the saints joins us to Christ, from whom as its fountain and head issues all graces, and the life of the People of God itself" (*CCC* 957).

How marvelous! I wonder if it might be a little like walking into that family reunion at my brother-in-law's house. Perhaps I'll see faces that are somehow familiar and yet somehow unfamiliar. Perhaps I won't recognize them at all—at least initially. But if we're all united in glory, it won't matter if I mistake a niece for a sister-in-law.

## What does Scripture say?

*I have heard of your faith in the Lord Jesus and your love toward all the saints, and for this reason I do not cease to give thanks for you as I remember you in my prayers. I pray that the God of our Lord Jesus Christ, the Father of glory, may give you a spirit of wisdom and revelation as you come to know him, so that, with the eyes of your heart enlightened, you may know what is the hope to which he has called you, what are the riches of his glorious inheritance among the saints...*

EPHESIANS 1:15–18

## What does my heart say?

I Are there any saints to whom I can relate?
I What kind of relationship do I have with him, her, or them?
I What is my understanding of sainthood?

❚ ❚ ❚ ❚

# IMMACULATE CONCEPTION
## Panagia

IN THE EASTERN RITE tradition of the Catholic Church, Mary is referred to as *Panagia*, the "All-holy" one. What an incredible term; she's not just *holy*, she's *all* holy! That implies that she's not only holy because of her words and actions, not only because of her obedience to God's will, not only because of her spirit of service and humility, but because of her very being.

The Dogmatic Constitution on the Church [*Lumen Gentium*], describes the concept like this:

> *It is no wonder then that it was customary for the holy Fathers to refer to the mother of God as all holy and free from every stain of sin, as though fashioned by the holy Spirit and formed as a new creature. Enriched from the first instant of her conception with the splendor of an entirely unique holiness, the virgin from Nazareth is hailed by the heralding angel, by divine command, as 'full of grace' (see Luke 1:28), and to the heavenly messenger she replies: 'Behold the handmaid of the Lord, be it done to me according to your word' (Luke 1:38). Thus the daughter of Adam, Mary, consenting to the word of God, became the Mother of Jesus. Committing herself whole-heartedly to God's saving will and impeded by no sin, she devoted herself totally, a handmaid of the Lord, to the person and work of her Son, under and with him, serving the mystery of redemption, by the grace of Almighty God. Rightly, therefore, the holy Fathers see Mary not merely as a passive instrument in the hands of God, but as freely cooperating in the work of human salvation through faith and obedience.*

Mary was so pure, so spotless, so holy that it was as though she was fashioned by the Holy Spirit and formed as a new creature. Isn't that amazing? She was (is) completely free of sin and yet completely human in every other regard.

I wonder what that might have looked like on a day-to-day basis. In her humble life at Nazareth, for example, how did she experience the trials and frustrations of caring for a family, living in poverty, carrying exhausting workloads, dealing with difficult relatives, friends and neighbors, and at the same time constantly discerning God's will in all things? Perhaps she didn't experience these things as trials and frustrations at all.

That's sure not the case in my own life. Every family crisis sends me into a tizzy. It's hard not to complain under the stress of long hours and yard-long lists of things to do. Every hurtful comment makes me want to lash back, and injustice (real or perceived) makes me entirely indignant. I can't even count the number of times a week I find myself asking God "why" and wanting to resist doing his will. Seems to me that my human sinfulness gets in the way of just about everything.

Because of her immaculate conception, Mary doesn't have the same tendencies toward sins and failings as you and I. I can imagine her responding to pain, stress, confusion and fatigue with a joyful "yes." However, her immaculate conception—and through that, her worthiness to bear the Savior—gives her the right and ability to intercede and intervene for us in our own shortcomings.

She's formed as a *new creature*. That means she experienced the same pain, confusion, frustrations and fatigue that we do. She handled them differently because she was able to see God's hand behind all things and therefore was void of the tendency to fight against his will.

As a kid, I used to think the immaculate conception was an unfair deal. If Mary was free of sin, why couldn't we be free, too? How come she got the advantage? Growing deeper in my faith, I came to realize that my logic was faulty. Of course she was free of sin. How could our Lord be conceived in the womb of anyone who was *not* all-holy?

Therefore, we all can rejoice with our Eastern Rite followers in proclaiming Mary the *Panagia*—the All-holy one—for her holiness far excels what we might achieve ourselves.

## What does Scripture say?

> *Have mercy on me, O God,*
> *according to your steadfast love;*
> *according to your abundant mercy*
> *blot out my transgressions.*
> *Wash me thoroughly from my iniquity,*
> *and cleanse me from my sin.*
> *For I know my transgressions,*
> *and my sin is ever before me.*
> *Against you, you alone, have I sinned,*
> *and done what is evil in your sight,*
> *so that you are justified in your sentence*
> *and blameless when you pass judgment.*
> *Indeed, I was born guilty,*
> *a sinner when my mother conceived me.*

PSALM 51:1–5

## What does my heart say?

**I** What does the word "holy" mean to me?
**I** How do I recognize holiness in another person?
**I** How can I become holy in my own life?

# Father Joseph Kentenich

■ ■ ■ ■ ■ ■ ■ ■ ■ ■ ■ ■ ■ ■ ■ ■ ■ ■ ■ ■ ■ ■ ■ ■ ■ ■ ■ ■ ■ ■ ■ ■ ■

FATHER JOSEPH KENTENICH was born in Gymnich, Germany, in 1885. At the age of nine, he consecrated himself to the Mother of God and was ordained a Pallotine Father in 1910. Shortly thereafter, he became the spiritual director of the seminarians at the Pallotine Seminary in Schoenstatt, Germany. With daring trust in divine providence, he founded The Apostolic Movement of Schoenstatt and Schoenstatt Shrine by sealing a covenant of love with the Mother Thrice Admirable of Schoenstatt in 1914.

From 1941–1945, Father Kentenich was interned by the Gestapo in the prison in Coblenz and the concentration camp in Dachau, where he endured unspeakable hardships and yet acted as a beacon of light for those imprisoned with him. He bore the hardships and degradation of the camp with great fortitude and joyful resignation, becoming a source of support and encouragement for his fellow prisoners. He worked in the service of the Mother Thrice Admirable throughout his ordeal and returned to Schoenstatt at the end of the war to resume his work for the movement.

From 1949–1965, he was separated from his work and sent to Milwaukee, Wisconsin, as a test by the Vatican to determine whether or not the Schoenstatt Movement was truly a work of God. During his exile, Father Kentenich proved his love and loyalty for both the Church and the Schoenstatt Movement with joyful endurance. Upon his reinstatement, he vivaciously returned to his work in Schoenstatt, Germany, where he died in 1968. He had devoted his entire life to the mission of the Mother Thrice Admirable, Queen and Victress of Schoenstatt.